INCLUSIVE PARTICIPATION OF LOCAL GOVERNMENTS IN MINDANAO PEACE:
Shaping Agendas & Ensuring Sustainability

Hazelyn A. Gaudiano

INCLUSIVE PARTICIPATION OF LOCAL GOVERNMENTS IN MINDANAO PEACE:
Shaping Agendas & Ensuring Sustainability

GALDA VERLAG 2023

Originally presented as the author's Master's thesis:
Notre Dame University, Cotabato City (Philippines), 2019

ISBN 978-3-96203-330-9 (Print)
ISBN 978-3-96203-331-6 (E-Book)

Bibliografische Information der Deutschen Nationalbibliothek
Die Deutsche Nationalbibliothek verzeichnet diese Publikation in der Deutschen
Nationalbibliografie; detaillierte bibliografische Daten sind im Internet über
https://www.dnb.de/

© 2023 Galda Verlag, Glienicke
Neither this book nor any part may be reproduced or transmitted in any form or by any means
electronic or mechanical, including photocopying, micro-filming, and recording, or by any
information storage or retrieval system, without prior permission in writing from the publisher.
Direct all inquiries to Galda Verlag, Franz-Schubert-Str. 61, 16548 Glienicke, Germany

ABSTRACT

The agreement between the MILF and the Government of the Philippines was intended to be one of the peacebuilding strategy to end the centuries-old problem of the Bangsamoro, and achieve a long lasting peace in Mindanao. Consequently, the effectiveness of a peace process, and the quality and sustainability of the agreement will be strengthened if we make the peacebuilding mechanisms inclusive and broaden the participation in the process itself. In general, the participation of the Local Government Units have observed to be untapped, and lagged – so their capacities, experiences, perspective, leadership, and potential are not being utilize. This study examines the inclusive participation of the LGUs in the peace process, in particular, in the GPH-MILF negotiation. In this paper also, brief narration of experiences and challenges of the LGUs have been documented, as well as how they were able to shape their agendas through activating new and existing alliances and inter-LGU coordination in the pursuit of a workable Bangsamoro Government. More so than the overall involvement, their dominant assertions on their roles and significant contribution to the peace process are also being presented. As a result, the study shows the diverse and complex ways of LGUs form of political participation – from creating social movements and dialogues, involvement in consultations, and activating and used of new and existing networks, to lobbying of their agenda through direct and indirect access to the negotiating table. Nonetheless, LGUs' visualizes the creation of a Bangsamoro government as a positive expression of achieving greater autonomy for the Bangsamoro to exercise their right to self- determination, with this, they have grasped any methodologies to push for their agenda. The logical and representative inclusion of LGUs in both parallel and horizontal lens of peace and security issues in the country, particularly in Mindanao peace process, is not exclusively essential in safeguarding a successful negotiation, but also for guaranteeing that the LGUs' interests are being addressed.

ACKNOWLEDGEMENT

To the people who have lent a hand to me in the development and materialization of this research output, I am wholeheartedly thankful to all of you.

I would first like to thank my thesis advisor Prof. Rey Danilo C. Lacson of the Institute for Autonomy and Governance (IAG). The door to Prof. Lacson office was always open whenever I ran into a trouble spot or had a question about my research or writing. He consistently allowed this paper to be my own work, but steered me in the right direction whenever he thought I needed it.

I would also like to thank the experts who were involved in the validation of the output for this research project: Dr. Alfred Taboada, Dr. Alano Kadil and Prof. Moh'd Asnin Pendatun. Without their passionate participation and input, the validation of the research output could not have been successfully conducted.

I would also like to acknowledge Dr. Ma. Theresa P. Llano, as the second reader of this paper, and I am gratefully indebted to her for her very valuable comments on this thesis.

A very special gratitude goes out to the Department of Foreign Affairs and Trade – Australia for helping and providing the funding for my study and my thesis. As well as, to Ustadz Mahmod Ahmad of the Bangsamoro Leadership and Management Institute (BLMI) for the trust and support in endorsing me as a recipient of the In-Country Scholarship Program 2 (ICSP 2).

To the participants of this research - the local chief executives and officials of the LGUs in Maguindanao, the Provincial Office of the Governor, OPAPP – Mindanao sub- office, Bangsamoro Transition Commissioners and Regional Legislative Assembly – for giving valuable time and patience to answer the research questions during interview.

To Dr. Theresa O. Corcoro, the Dean of the Graduate School, for her unrelenting support and encouragement during the course of my study.

Finally, I must express my very profound gratitude to my IAG colleagues, to my friends and most especially to my family for providing me with unfailing support and continuous encouragement throughout my years of study, and through the process of researching and writing this research paper. This accomplishment would not have been possible without them.

To all those I failed to mention but were instrumental in making this work done. Above all to the Almighty God for the gift of wisdom. Thank you.

HAZELYN A. GAUDIANO, RN
Researcher

CONTENTS

Abstract v
Acknowledgement vii
Figures xiii
Tables xxi

1 Introduction 1

Related Literature 2

The Moro people and the struggle for self-determination in brief historical perspective 3
The Local Government Unit and its mandate 5
Treatment Accorded to the ARMM 6
Inclusive participation in the peace process 7
GPH-MILF Peace Agreement 8
Bangsamoro Government — Local Government Units Relations 9
LGUs involvement in the GPH-MILF Peace Process 10

Conceptual Framework 13

Statement of the Problem 15

Significance of the Study 16

Operational Definition of Terms 17

2 Methods 19

Design 19

Participants 19

Setting 20

Procedure 20

Limitations of the Study.. 21

3 Results and Discussions.. 27

Participants' Profile... 27

LGUs involvement in the GPH-MILF peace process 28

Maguindanao LGU Perspectives.. 28

From the Bangsamoro Transition Commission
perspective 32

Experiences and Challenges in the Peace Process......................... 36

Inter-LGU Coordination Mechanisms 41

Dominant Assertions on the need for LGUs' political
participation 46

Implications... 51

4 Summary 55

Conclusion... 57

Recommendations... 58

Recommendations for Further Studies... 60

APPENDICES 63

REFERENCES 79

FIGURES

FIGURE 1   Comparison of the number of consultations of various stakeholders with LGUs from 2010–2015 11

FIGURE 2   Four Pillars of LGUs' inclusive political participation in the peace process 14

TABLES

TABLE 1 Number of Consultation Activities with LGU of ARMM from 2010-2015..........................13

TABLE 2 Selected Characteristics of the Participants.......28

1
INTRODUCTION

After more than a decade of negotiations, the peace panels of both the Government of the Republic of the Philippines (GPH) and of the Moro Islamic Liberation Front (MILF) have come to an agreement on how the centuries-old problem of the Bangsamoro may be addressed. "The twists and turns, as some political analyst describes the way the talks have been moving, have even stalled at times, leaving the peace process in a state of suspended animation" (Bacani, 2008). Countless methodologies and approaches were grasped by the different administrations, from talking peace and development to all-out war and back to peace and development again. In all these, the aspect of governance is not being emphasized in all formulations of the analysis.

Understanding the importance of local governance to the body politic in the Mindanao Peace Process have never been perceived. In this latest chapter of the peace negotiation, governance has been given significance, but more in terms of the relationship between the national and regional government (Tayao, 2017). However, its link to the Local Government Units (LGUs) and their capacity for the peacebuilding initiatives and efforts should also be considered and be heeded.

According to Meen (2017), peace needs a collective effort. Everyone needs to collaborate with the government and other stakeholders to ensure the people live in peace. Consequently, during the inauguration speech of President Rodrigo Duterte on June 2016, he mentioned the call for the participation of all other stakeholders, among others, to ensure inclusivity in the peace process. By means of a peaceful political climate in the region, it ensures the sustainability of the Mindanao peace process and the effective implementation of resulting agreements — but it is contingent to the crucial support of the LGUs, as well as the local political power gatekeepers. Likewise,

"...their informed participation in dialogues is just as crucial towards the incremental success of the broader peace process" (Lacson, 2017, Foreword section, para. 1).Tackling the issue does not just require specific groups and people to be involved. For the process to be effective, it needs to be inclusive and participatory. But what constitutes inclusive participation, and how can the Moro fronts, the Bangsamoro people, the negotiators and the Government of the Philippines achieve lasting peace in Mindanao?

The life and rhythm of the evolving Mindanao Peace Process would solely depend on the inclusive political participation of each sector — for the LGUs, their participation remained being documented as underlining their essential "back room" roles they play in linking boundaries and supporting those formally engaged in peace negotiations. Drawing on discussions, interviews and, review of literature, this study looks at the experiences of the LGUs and explains how critical their inclusive participation is to the process. Moreover, study will examine the inclusive participation of local government in the process and to understand much more about how local government units works, and thereby initiate the search for the imperative options to achieve an optimally working peace process. This study would like to look into the Local Government Units' (LGUs) inclusive participation in peace negotiations. Providing an overview on how they have been involved and engaged in the broader lens of peacemaking in the country, particularly their participation in the Bangsamoro peace process of the GPH-MILF talks.

Related Literature

Over the time, the review of the significance of Local Government Units' (LGUs) inclusive participation in peace and development agenda in Mindanao, particularly in the formal and/or high-level of peace negotiation came in two streams. Within the first stream framework, the observation conceptualizes the LGUs addressing a myriad of conflicts and peace issues—their"...experiences of conflict, then, extends beyond peace and order concerns to include poverty (conflict over wealth and resources), gender violence, and other forms of structural violence" (UNDP-OPAPP Guidebook on CSPP Local Development Planning, 2013); and reflects LGUs as peacebuilders in the local level and the nature of LGUs mandate as local community gatekeepers for conflict prevention and conflict resolution. In particular, this body of the review focuses on the LGUs potent role on community organizing and participation in informal peace negotiations, underlining their essential "backroom" roles they play in linking boundaries and supporting those formally engaged in peace negotiations. The second stream of review, produced after the recognition of the significance of governance in the later peace process, but more in terms of the relationship between the national and regional government. In particular, the recognition of the LGUs' capacity and its relationship with the regional government should be strengthened (Tayao, 2017).

The Moro people and the struggle for self-determination in brief historical perspective

"The story of the Moro people's struggle for self-determination is a story of a people's struggle against attempt of assimilation into the wider body politic of the Philippine society" (Mercado, 1999). Arguably, it is the longest in Asia and maybe the whole world, it started in the 16th century and up to now there is no clear indicator yet as to when it will end (Alim, 2000). Other peoples' struggle in the world has either prospered or being totally crumpled. While in the Philippines, the struggle for cultural identity, survival and the right to self-determination is a continuing struggle for the Moro (Alim, 2000).

The pursuit of the Moro to build their own autonomous government is hinged on the people's unrelenting definition and re-definition of their national identity (Buendia, 2008). The Moro people consider themselves as the unconquered people of the Philippines. Their struggle for self-determination dates back to 1565 — a struggle that is not an isolated cry of the religious community in quest of their accommodation within the framework of the Philippine society, but like any ethnic minorities, it is a struggle of a people craving the right to be the foci of their own land (Mercado, 1999).

Called Moro by the Spaniards, which refer to the indigenous Islamized inhabitants in the Philippines alluding to the Muslim Moorish occupation of the Iberian Peninsula (Spain and Portugal) and the northern coast of the African continent in 711 A.D — thus in the 16th century, the Spaniards encountered the ferocious resistance of Muslims inhabiting the Southern Sultanates of the country in their attempt to colonize the archipelago. This prompted them of their prehistoric enemy, the Moors, thus called the Philippine Muslims Moros (Phelan 1959; Corpuz 1989).

Popularization of the word "Bangsamoro" came out of the mayhem of the late 1960s to the 1970s, during the rule of strongman Ferdinand E. Marcos (Lingga, 2016). Moro National Liberation Front (MNLF) chairman and organizer, Prof. Nur Misuari described that "Bangsamoro" denotes to both identity and the measure to allow those who recognized themselves as Moros — but over time, Bangsamoro emanated to signify the Moro homeland as well.

As a summary of the Bangsamoro aspiration for self-determination, the MNLF originally sought independence for Mindanao and the Sulu Archipelago (located southwest of mainland Mindanao) but accepted autonomy in 1976 as part of the Tripoli Agreement — the first such treaty between the government and a Moro rebel group (Lingga, 2016). The agreement has few provisions, but it reflects the Bangsamoro aspiration for self-determination—it provided for an autonomous area for Muslims in the southern Philippines. Unfortunately, during the Marcos regime (1977) the provisions of the agreement were preceded and implemented unilaterally—resulting to an establishment of too weak (and so- called) autonomous regions rather than one strong and truly autonomous region as envisaged in the accord (Buendia, 2012). The MNLF campaigned to discredit this arrangement whereby the Muslim population became part of two regions, Region XII in central Mindanao and the Region IX in Zamboanga Peninsula and the Sulu Archipelago (Lingga, 2016).

The foundational 1989 law for ARMM, Republic Act 6734, gave the autonomous region a political structure that takes over the country's presidential system. The 1996 Final Peace Agreement also conveyed the same political structure to the ARMM, and this was reflected in the new ARMM law (Republic Act 9054) passed in 2001 (see Lingga 2016; Alim 2000; Mercado1999 for a detailed account). Over the time, the MNLF led-secessionist struggle concluded, but pursued by the Moro Islamic Liberation Front –are now the most compelling armed organization trailing the Moro secessionist movement (Buendia, 2012).

Notwithstanding the ideological differences between the MNLF and MILF — the former as more secular while the latter being more Islamic — they see themselves as "one people." The perception of being one person separated from the bordering populaces, the Filipinos, Bangsamoro is expressed and self-ascribed, bound communally on the foundation of a shared origin, antiquity, culture, organizations, territory, and more outstandingly, religion (Buendia, 2012).

Fast-forward, the MILF enters into an agreement with the Philippine Government through a Comprehensive Agreement on the Bangsamoro (CAB), by contrast with the past peace pacts, it revisits the 1976 Tripoli Agreement. In particular, as cited in one of Lingga 2016 papers that,

> ... two of the core provisions are "the government of the Bangsamoro shall have a ministerial form" and "asymmetric" relationship with the central

government. It further endows the Bangsamoro government with greater control over its finances, with "creation of sources of revenue" an exclusive powers over budgeting, ancestral domain, and natural resources, land management and distribution, land reclassification, and in land waters.

Accordingly, in Buendia 2012 journal, the late MILF Chairman Hashim Salamat believed that the GRP-MNLF FPA only settled the government's problem and not the Bangsamoro problem, he further specified that "the agreement never touched the core of the Bangsamoro problem which is the illegal and immoral usurpation of their (referring to the Moros) ancestral homeland and legitimate rights to freedom and self-determination".

Additionally, to be able to assert the Moro's right to self-determination, majority of the aspects of the CAB itself necessitates its ratification through a Bangsamoro law that is an enabling measure for the replacement of the Autonomous Region in Muslim Mindanao with a more empowered Bangsamoro political entity (Lorena, 2017).

The Local Government Unit and its mandate

The LGU is part of the government that is closest to the people and is in the responsibility of providing basic services and facilities to its constituents. Under Section 15 of Republic Act 7160, otherwise known as the Local Government Code of 1991, defines "a Local Government Unit as a body politic and corporate endowed with powers to be exercised by it in conformity with law". As such, it executes dual functions, governmental and proprietary. The first function, which is governmental, focuses on the advancement of the public good or welfare by way of affecting the public generally such as in health, safety and security, and other community concerns (DPSLRU, 1961). On the other hand, the latter which is the proprietary functions are those that pursue to acquire special corporate benefits or gross monetary profit and projected for private gain and benefit (Blaquera v. Alcala, 1998). For instance, LGUs' can be an agency of the national government when performing governmental powers and executing governmental duties, nevertheless, they also act as an agent of the community in the administration of local affairs when engaged in corporate activities (Batas Pinoy, 2011).

LGUs in the country have four (4) classifications — provinces and independent cities, component cities and municipalities, barangays, and in one part, is an autonomous region — the Autonomous Region of Muslim Mindanao. Subsequently, LGUs are considered autonomous from the national government, in which each LGU has the right and the authority to normalize its undertakings — political, economic, social, and administrative — dependable with the national policies (CANA Primer, 2014).

In the Philippines, under its constitution, Section 2 and 4 of Article X, the local governments "shall enjoy genuine and meaningful local autonomy", and in which the president exercises "general supervision". In addition, the Article X known as the Local Government Code of the Philippines in 1991which was legislated by the congress will "provide for a more responsive and accountable local government structure instituted through a system of decentralization whereby Local Government Units shall be given more powers, authority, responsibilities, and resources. The process of decentralization shall proceed from the national government to the Local Government Units" (Article X LGC 1991, Declaration of Policy).

Basically, LGUs are composed of an elected barangay chairman, also known as the punong barangay; mayors and vice mayors for both municipalities and cities; governors and vice governors. They are the ones which head the executive department of their respective LGU. The residents also elect for their representatives to the Sanggunian or the council, the legislative branch of the LGU, and these are called Board Members at the provincial level, and councilors from the city and municipality to the barangay level (CANA Primer, 2014).

Treatment Accorded to the ARMM

Republic Act 6734 otherwise known as "An Act Providing for an Organic Act for the Autonomous Region in Muslim Mindanao" officially declares that the ARMM is an autonomous region constituting provinces, cities, and municipalities in Muslim Mindanao. Specifically, Article 3 Section 3 states, to wit:

> "The Regional Government shall adopt a policy on local autonomy whereby regional powers shall be devolved to local government units where appropriate: Provided, however, that until a regional law implementing this provision is enacted, the local Government Code shall be applicable."

In principle, the above stated section of the law clearly points to the character of the ARMM as larger than the Local Government Units, and should be treated as such. This text of the Organic Act is often invoked to support the argument that the ARMM is more than the Local Government Unit.

However, during the roundtable discussion facilitated by the Institute for Autonomy and Governance on April 2011, Atty. Naguib Sinarimbo pointed out that "ARMM is being treated merely as a local government unit, diluting its autonomous character" due to the national-regional relations, weak electoral system, poor access to and control of exploitation and utilization of strategic resources, weak fiscal autonomy, and poor delivery and access to basic services and facilities — which constitutes the ailments of the ARMM[1] (IAG, 2014).

Nonetheless, there is also an argument that says the ARMM is lesser than the Local Government Units. For one, no less than Senator Richard Gordon said, "I believe LGUs in other regions enjoy a higher degree of fiscal autonomy than those in the ARMM".[2] He forwarded this argument based on the reason that the share of the ARMM in the Internal Revenue collection is too small, "… as a leverage for the regional government to rally LGUs to help fulfill ARMM's mandate"[3] (Senate, 2007).

Inclusive participation in the peace process

The effectiveness of the peace process and the quality and sustainability of the agreement will be strengthened if we broaden the participation in the process itself and make the peacebuilding mechanisms inclusive (Paffenholz, 2014). However, it is also unclear what is meant by inclusivity and participation. According to the study on Women Leading Peace
2015, the discrepancy is due to both the varied understanding of indirect participation and direct participation, as well as the framework on which a writer shapes his/her argument—e.g., equality and rights, utility, social transformation (Chang, et.al. 2015).

In the same aforementioned literature review, participation refers to the action of taking part in something — thus, the varied activities that compromise participation include mobilization, activism, building an advocacy based social movement, forming coalitions, negotiation, mediation, standing for office, drafting legislation and formal agreements, holding implementers accountable, etc.

Tackling the problems and difficulties in the Mindanao peace process necessitates not only signed peace agreements but also sustainable peace. "It is not enough to bring armed actors to the negotiating table, however, to be effective, the peace process needs to be inclusive and participatory" (Rausch, Luu 2017). Successively, from Cambridge dictionary (2018), the other term,

---

[1] IAG 2011: Roundtable Discussion: What Ails ARMM?
[2] Senate Press Release 2007
[3] Ibid

which is "inclusivity", denotes the quality of trying to include many different types of people and treat them all fairly and equally. Accordingly, there are two dimensions of inclusivity, one it is identified both a practical dimension of inclusivity (inclusion as a tool for sustainable peace) and two, a more profound value dimension, which is often framed in normative terms - inclusion as a moral obligation, a question of fairness (Romo and Smeets 2015).

Based on the Conciliation Resources May 2015 Report,

> Peace negotiations often surpass the significance of other, more inclusive and democratic participation and decision-making processes that may be at least as significant, and yet incline to be considered only of secondary importance.
>
> Practice has shown time and again that a peace agreement cannot be implemented without broader ownership in society; and that actions to address structural and cultural violence need to develop beyond the negotiating table. (pp. 7)

In view of the presented body of literature on the inclusive peace process and inclusive participation — it is heightened to recognize that avital transferal is desirable to equilibrate the disproportionateness between the relevance of formal peace negotiations between armed actors, the government and the broader peace process that necessities to embrace society at large. In which, according to Rausch and Luu (2017), guaranteeing transparency and building channels for public participation can help legitimize the process.

GPH-MILF Peace Agreement

The Comprehensive Agreement on the Bangsamoro (CAB) between the Government of the Philippines (GPH) and the Moro Islamic Liberation Front (MILF) aims to craft a new governance framework that will more effectively realize autonomous self-governance for the Islamzed indigenous peoples, or Moros, in Mindanao. "Issues of constitutionality, inclusivity, transparency, and acceptability have made the crafting of a political settlement difficult and contentious" (Ferrer, 2016). However, on March 27, 2014, after seventeen years of protracted negotiations, culminated in the signing of the peace pact.

Consequently, the CAB signifies the first substantial peace agreement worldwide in ten years and has turned out to be a foreseeable source for any other contemporary peace process (Herbolzheimer, 2015). It is a testament to the perseverance of the Philippine government and the MILF in reaching a political settlement. Not just one document, it is composed of all agreements entered into by the government and the MILF since 1997, when negotiations began, up to 2014, when the last annex, or supplemental agreement, to the Framework Agreement on the Bangsamoro was inked (Lingga, 2016).

The pact would create an autonomous Bangsamoro political entity (Knack, 2014) that is to substitute the current Autonomous Region in Muslim Mindanao (ARMM) and allow the MILF to demobilize as an armed group and to take part in elections and governance (Ferrer, 2016).

For decades, Bangsamoros have appealed for genuine autonomy, decrying the inadequacies of the arrangements they were previously given. The CAB promises to give them this, but it still faces a major challenger, including its translation into a law by the Philippine legislature and the realities on the ground in Muslim Mindanao, the area that will be encompassed by the Bangsamoro (Lingga, 2016).

Bangsamoro Government — Local Government Units Relations

The constitutional status of local government plays a significant role in a way it can cope with contemporary issues and in the freedom it has from central control (Copus, 2013). Consequently, in the proposed Bangsamoro Government, one of the foremost disquiets was the relationship between the Bangsamoro entity and the LGUs within its territorial jurisdiction. For MILF, a weakness in the current ARMM is its lack of effective control over the LGUs. LGUs undeniably enjoy better access to national central government's internal revenue allotment — in which the regional government, by contrast, has to haggle to Congress for its annual budget. The LGUs in the ARMM are also beneath the prerogative of the national Department of Interior and Local Government (DILG), by which the governors with good access can in fact go straight to Malacañang for additional funds — and, for all intents and purposes, bypass and ignore the ARMM (Ferrer, 2016). With this, the MILF position principally is that the Bangsamoro through a Bangsamoro law and succeeding statute can restructure its integral units and excerpt liability and a measure of control over the LGUs.

For Ampatuan 2015, during the IAG-UNDP Roundtable Discussion Series on Muslim Mindanao Autonomy in Senate, it became a problem in the negotiation on how to deal with the issue of the LGUs because there is the Local Government Code of 1991 that practically empowered the local chief executives and the LGUs in the country, including the ARMM. He further added that there was a dilemma on how to reconcile the LGUs in the Bangsamoro since many provisions in the original ARMM Organic Law were not reflected in the Local Government Code of 1991 thereby giving rise to a situation where substantial powers were devolved to the LGUs but at the same time limiting devolution of these powers to the ARMM itself.

In the same RTD, it was explained that because of the two-tiered devolution, some LGUs felt that the ARMM is simply another tier of the bureaucracy which in effect hampered the exercise of the autonomy granted to them. To solve this, it was proposed during the negotiations to empower the Bangsamoro regional government so that it can, in turn, give more to the LGUs in its jurisdiction. In which, the key principle pertaining to the relationship between the Bangsamoro regional government and the LGUs is that the LGUs are constituent units of the Bangsamoro — as such, the regulation of the powers would have to be transferred to the Bangsamoro regional government on the assumption that more powers should be given to it that it can effectively devolve further powers to the LGUs.

In another consultation in 2014, the LGUs are holding their hope to the approaching legislation for the Bangsamoro, expressing that the Basic Law must be able to convey real autonomy this time around, a mission its forerunner — Republic Act 9054 or the Amended Organic Act of the ARMM — came short. They share the understanding that autonomy in the ARMM is a failure relatively because of incomplete devolution (IAG, 2014). The LGUs avowed that more powers and authorities should have been devolved by the national government to the ARMM regional government, and by the ARMM regional government to local governments. A circumstance in fact is the provision of services in the education and health sector, and a function currently exercised by the regional government that should have been devolved to LGUs.

Nevertheless, the LGUs view the creation of the Bangsamoro as largely optimistic, but intimated at the same time that the negotiating panels should have consulted with them more closely by requiring their representation in the negotiating table. However, as observed from the roundtable series of IAG in 2014, the feeling of being left out and not being closely consulted is not simmering into a palpable dissatisfaction (IAG, 2014).

LGUs involvement in the GPH-MILF Peace Process

To date, there are only few existing published literature on explaining in details the ways in which LGUs' contributed to the peace process, thus, highlighting their effective roles in espousing a consensus-based approach to shaping an agenda, piloted internal peace and local security challenges through extensive dialogue, formed strategic alliances with other LGUs and sectors in the area, lobbied persistently to advance their goals, and maintaining their supportive and "backroom roles" in the process. Local government units have a long history of peace works in the Philippines –the earliest documented examples of LGUs' political initiatives date back on the enactment of the Local Government Code of 1991 which provided for a more responsive and accountable local government structure instituted through a system of decentralization (Article X LGC 1991, Declaration of Policy) of powers, responsibilities, and resources directly related to organization and operations of its local government, thus, peace and local security aspects are attached. Consequently, peace-building as a matter of national importance was institutionalized with the ratification of Executive Order No. 3 by President Gloria Macapagal-Arroyo, on February 28, 2001. E.O. No. 3, entitled "Defining Policy and Administrative Structure for Government's Peace Efforts" positioned the context for the implementation, coordination, monitoring, and integration of all government peace initiatives in the search of a just and lasting peace in the country (OPAPP-UNDP, 2013).

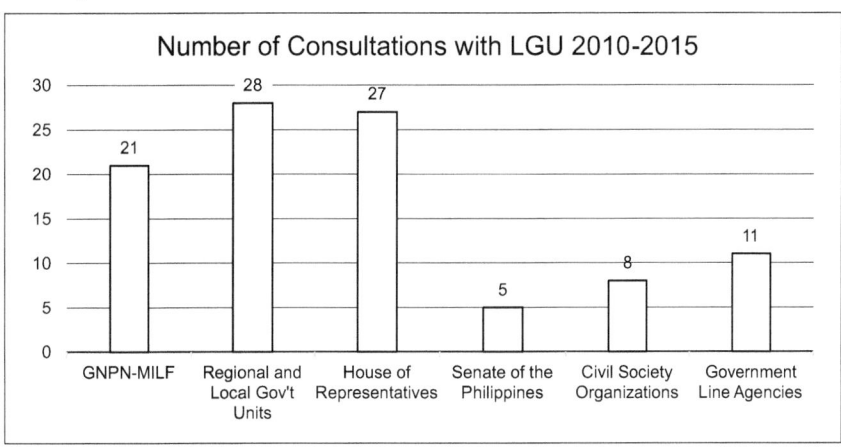

Source: OPAPP 2015

FIGURE 1   Comparison of the number of consultations of various stakeholders with LGUs from 2010–2015

Consequently, the Government of the Philippines (GPH) peace panel conducted and participated in 553 consultations among the various stakeholders of the Bangsamoro peace process from 2010 up until the completion of the

Comprehensive Agreement on the Bangsamoro (CAB) and the drafting of the proposed Bangsamoro Basic Law (BBL) (OPAPP, 2016).Out of these, there are one-hundred (100) documented activities participated and conducted by the leaders and officials of local government units, and with initiatives from the negotiating panel — OPAPP and various government and non-government stakeholders (see Figure 1). The figures are from the Office of the Presidential Adviser for Peace Process (OPAPP) position paper submitted to the Senate Committee on Local Government on 18 May 2015, likewise, the consultation activities such as meetings, workshops, fora, and briefings are initiatives by the government negotiating panel and other various stakeholders in order to shed light on the developments in the peace process with the MILF as well as to share and gather information, positions, and insights from the various stakeholders.

In the table, consultation activities were organized by the different stakeholders within the Bangsamoro core territory and the adjacent provinces, 21 activities were conducted by the GPNP-MILF/OPAPP, 28 were initiatives by the regional government of ARMM, particularly sessions of the RLA, and also both from the provincial and local government units of ARMM and contiguous areas, 27 were the public hearings conducted by the House of Representatives, 5 from the Senate of the Philippines, which were mostly carried out during the deliberation of the BBL in the upper house, 8 documented consultation activities were conducted by the civil society groups such as local NGOs and from the academe, and 11 activities were organized by the different national line agencies such as the Local Government Academy (LGA) of the DILG and the Philippine Army.

Some of the consultations were also an LGU led activity and have invited representatives from the GPNP-MILF/OPAPP to help them understand the whole Bangsamoro agenda, particularly, to voice out their positions, insights, and suggestions relative to the peace efforts with the MILF. Aside from that, LGU remains to be consistently active in conducting local activities that would support the peace process to move forward, and these activities were either in collaboration with various stakeholders (such as local non- government organizations and international organizations), from the directives coming from the Office of the Provincial Governor, and a simple initiative coming from the local chief executive of that LGU.

Consequently, the case of the Philippines is one of the few instances where sectoral representatives are voluntarily leading and contributing substantively in the formal negotiations — for LGUs, it is believe that their participation and representation have not been sought. However, the question is, how LGUs' mobilize for peace, gained access, and have leveraged their articulations in the Bangsamoro discourse? How the LGU in ARMM raised their positions and concerns to the crafted Bangsamoro law? And how the LGU of Maguindanao and BTC locate the participation of the LGU in the peace process? To link any nuances, Table 2 presents the number of the consultation with LGU conducted in ARMM, regardless of the organizing committee, from the time of negotiations in 2010 to the public consultations of the BBL in 2015. The figures in the table are also from the OPAPP 2015 data, however, numbers also cannot assure the participants of the study were invited and/or participated in the consultations. In summary, there are 6 consultations happened during 2010-2011 with 2 consultations from Maguindanao, then another 13 were organized from 2012-2013, and 21 consultations conducted in 2014-2015 — the time when the draft Bangsamoro law is in both in the upper and lower houses.

TABLE 1   Number of Consultation Activities with LGU of ARMM from 2010-2015

Province	2010-2011	2012-2013	2014-2015
Maguindanao	2	3	3
Lanao del Sur	1	1	6
Basilan	1	1	3
Sulu	1	3	5
Tawi-Tawi	1	0	3
RLA and ARMM (ORG)	0	5	1
Total	6	13	21

Source: OPAPP (2015)

Conceptual Framework

The body of literature on the Local Government Units' inclusive participation in peacemaking remains nascent. Accordingly, inclusion in a peace process for all groups affected by a conflict, and in the future governance of a country, is an important tool in ending conflicts (Suazo, 2013).

In the Philippines, the problems that hampered the implementation of past peace agreements highlight the need for a collective ownership of the peace process and its results by the involved local governments. Though, it is generally understood that to achieve a long lasting peace in the country, the process should involve wide spectrum of actors — as such, in underpinning an inclusive political process - the study utilizes four (4) pillars of participation as specified in the research objective, namely: involvement of the LGUs in the peace process, their experiences and challenges, inter-LGU alliances/coordination mechanisms and LGUs' assertion on the need for political participation. The frame of analysis anchors on Structural Functionalism Theory.

Structural functionalism is a sociological theory that attempts to explain why society functions the way it does by focusing on the relationships between the various social institutions that make up society (Macionis and Gerber, 2010). Following the principles of Structural Functionalism, the inclusive participation of the Local Government Units in the peace negotiations and peacemaking in the GPH-MILF peace process will manifest and validate the understanding that society is a complex system whose parts work together to promote solidarity and stability.

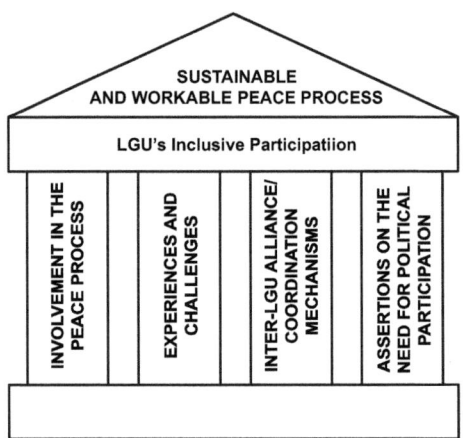

FIGURE 2   Four Pillars of LGUs' inclusive political participation in the peace process

Basically, the argument of the study posits that the four (4) pillars of LGUs' successful inclusive political participation serve to buttress a sustainable and workable peace process, collectively, these pillar work as working whole. This postulate leads to the principle that all structures and functions are necessary for a successful inclusive political participation of LGUs, and in order to achieve a sustainable peace and development in Mindanao. Just as this structure or institutions contribute to the maintenance of other parts of the Mindanao social system — the four (4) pillars complete the interrelated parts moving the broader Mindanao peace process forward.

The achievement of the workable and sustainable Mindanao peace, specifically anchors on the implementation process and the implementation actor. The lead implementation actor of political agreements is the LGU. It is the LGU who will be tasked to realize and substantiate whatever provisions are provided in the final agreement. In the post agreement scenario, "implementation" is synonymous with LGU action.

In principle, implementers are necessary participants to the drafting process to ensure that the details of the implementation process are understood and faithfully executed. This is where the participation of LGU in the peace process is highly crucial and fundamental towards the achievement of the workable Mindanao peace. This necessitates the pillars of LGU participation: a) involvement of the LGUs in the peace process; b) their experiences and challenges; c) inter-LGU alliances/coordination mechanisms; and d) LGUs' assertion on the need for political participation.

Statement of the Problem

The study aims to examine the Local Government Units' participation in the GPH- MILF peace process. Specifically, the study seeks to answer the following questions:

1) How are the LGUs' involved in the GPH-MILF Peace Process?
2) What are the prevailing experiences and challenges of the Local Government Units' participation in the peace negotiations?
3) How does inter-LGU coordination influence in terms of asserting their participation in the peace process?
4) What are the dominant assertions on the need for LGUs' political participation in the peace process?
5) What are the emerging analyses connecting the need for the LGUs' involvement in the political and formal peace negotiations towards local peace policy formulation?

Significance of the Study

The capacity to govern locally does not necessarily translate into the right knowledge, skill sets and a mandate to engage in peace processes at the regional or national level (Menkhaus, 2014). However, what shapes a successful peace process is an all-inclusive participation among all stakeholders existing in the core territory. Consequently, the study focuses on the Local Government Units' inclusive participation in the GPH-MILF peace process. This study can generate inputs to the formulation of policy actions and the appropriate peace building approaches to support efforts in achieving a desired inclusive peace in the Bangsamoro. Furthermore, the knowledge produced by the study is also a contribution to the continuing discourse on peace building.

Specifically, for the LGUs, the study will help substantiate the formulation of local peace policies for the institutionalization of their direct participation in the evolving Mindanao peace process. For the negotiators, the study can be an added reference to its formulation in the Bangsamoro agenda, taking into account the LGUs' capacity and roles playing with their relationship both with the regional and national government. For the OPAPP, the study can inform its policy actions toward facilitating an inclusive peace in the country. For the policy maker, to access and use the suggested formulated research policy to strengthen the direct participation of the LGUs, as well as to empower other stakeholders for a more inclusive process. For the government alone, knowledge and insights from the study can help them build more responsive governance parallel with the significance of participatory governance and an inclusive political process.

Furthermore, to the future Bangsamoro Government, results and recommendations of the study can be adopted to help strengthen the formulation of provisions and policy that would support in creating a sustainable and workable government. Finally, to other countries who have been currently working their own peace process, lessons learned from the research findings and from all the narratives of the participants in total can help them recognized the significance of inclusivity, particularly counting the political sectors to include their priorities codified in the peace agreements that ultimately pave the way for the next chapter in the histories of a meaningful and legitimate peace process.

Operational Definition of Terms

For the purpose of adding clarity to the approach taken in this paper, the following definitions of key concepts are used:

Bangsamoro — It refers to both identity and the movement to free those who identifies themselves as Moros (a group of Islamized people). The term also denotes the Moro homeland.

Governance — the exercise of economic, political and administrative authority to manage a country's affairs at all levels. It comprises the mechanisms, processes and institutions through which citizens and groups articulate their interests, exercise their legal rights, meet their obligations and mediate their differences (UNDP, 1997)

Inclusive Participation — It refers to the broader ownership of the process among stakeholders, in particular, it signifies the direct participation of all people and/or representative of each sector in the society in both formal and informal peace process.

Local Government Unit — an LGU as a body politic and corporate endowed with powers to be exercised by it in conformity with law. As such, it performs dual functions, governmental and proprietary (Section 15 of Republic Act 7160, LGC 1991).

Peace Process — a political process in which conflict are resolved by peaceful means — through negotiations, mediation, dialogue in both official and unofficial arenas. (Saunders, 1999)

Right of Self-Determination — collective right of peoples to determine their own future free of any outside interference or coercion. It includes the right to determine their political status and to freely pursue their economic, social, spiritual and cultural development (Lingga, 2002).

2
METHODS

Design

The study employed largely the qualitative method which was built primarily on testimonies from first-hand interviews and focus group discussions of key people in the Local Government Units' in Bangsamoro core territories, as well as negotiators both from the GPH and MILF peace panel, in addition to a review of existing literature. A basic quantitative approach was utilized in the initial determination of the demographic profile of the Participants. The interviews were qualitative, in-depth, semi-structured and open-ended, and is used to gather information from a range of relevant actors about their perspectives on the LGUs' inclusive participation in the countries post-conflict political processes.

Participants

The participants of the study included a variety of LGUs' structure at the regional, provincial and municipal level — thus, it involved some of the Local Chief Executives (LCEs), provincial and municipal administrative officers, Municipal Local Government Operation Officers (MLGOO), provincial board members, league of municipality of mayors, representatives from the Regional Legislative Assembly (RLA), and other key persons in the province and municipality.

With limited time and resources, firsthand information was collected from a diverse sample of 12 local government unit structure, including officials from the executive and legislative branch. The executive branch includes the mayors, administrative officers, MLGOO and some technical staff and officials working under the executive committee, while, on the other hand, the study also interviewed members from the legislative branch namely: representatives from the RLA, Vice mayors and Sangguniang Bayan. The data were collected through semi-structured interviews to obtain deep insights and rich information.

Where possible, representatives from the Bangsamoro Transition Commission (BTC) and OPAPP that participated in the peace negotiations were interviewed as well. The criteria used in the selection: recognized as political, moral leaders, with broad knowledge of the Bangsamoro conflict and peace dynamics.

Setting

The study took place in Cotabato City with travel to adjacent province — and conducted within the Bangsamoro core territory, particularly in the Autonomous Region in Muslim Mindanao (ARMM) mainland province, the Maguindanao. It covered and generated results from the twelve (12) LGU structures namely, the municipalities of Datu Odin Sinsuat, Sultan Mastura, Matanog, Sultan Kudarat, Datu Anggal Midtimbang, Talayan, Ampatuan, Shariff Aguak, Datu Montawal, Mangudadatu, Datu Saudi Ampatuan, and Guindulungan, as well as, from the ARMM regional office in Cotabato City and the Maguindanao provincial office in Buluan, Maguindanao. With this, accessibility, local peace and security situation, and early confirmation from the LGUs have been the considerations for selecting the municipalities involved.

Procedure

A purposive sampling method was used to identify study participants. The researcher connected with known personalities who have personal or professional links with the identified participants of the study. Request letters for interview were sent, and direct personal contacts were established to secure an appointment. Interview schedules were sent after they gave their consent to become one of the participants of the key informant interviews. For a focus group discussion, same consent and request letters were sent to the identified key people for sessions' schedule and discussions. Interview responses were electronically recorded, and transcribed in full. See Appendix B for the flow chart of the research data collection and procedure.

During the preliminary interaction with each potential participant, the researcher expounded the nature and purpose of the study, and seek voluntary participation. Where necessary, communication and questions were translated into the local language.

To guarantee reliability and validity of the results, the numerous sources were triangulated to cross-validate the degree of consistency against the mainstream literature. Nonconformities from the mainstream literature were reconciled and new information was evaluated and specified in the result. Interview quotes and connotations were confirmed with member authorizations to ensure accuracy. Furthermore, the design of the study was observant to ethical considerations. In particular, the study was conducted on the basis of voluntary participation and a principle of *do no harm*. The confidentiality of the participants was strictly guaranteed throughout the data collection, analysis, and report writing stages. All interview participants that permitted the public identification of their name and/or organization are properly quoted in the results and discussions of the study.

Limitations of the Study

The study is limited to determining the prevailing experiences and challenges of the LGUs inclusive participation in the peace negotiations, as well as to examine their nature of involvement, extent of influence in political decision-making in the evolving GPH-MILF peace process. Still, it was focused on identifying dominant assertions on the need for the LGUs' political participation in the process, additionally, the evolving strategies of their inter-LGU coordination. Furthermore, the study is only limited to the existing LGUs in the Province of Maguindanao.

Consequently, the study samples four (4) participant categories based on the individual's level of participation and involvement in the peace process: (1) representatives from the BTC or negotiating panel, (2) leaders in the local government unit — its' local chief executive and second highest elected and appointed member in the unit, (3) government officials that participated in the peace negotiations- from the regional and provincial governments who have been involved and participated in any peace process discourse and consultation organized by the government agencies and non-government organizations in support to the peace negotiations, and (4) from the OPAPP.

More so than that, the study is only limited to the LGUs participation and were not able to capture other sectors in terms of their involvement and participation in the GPH-MIF Peace Process.

The study was conducted from November to March 2018.

3
RESULTS AND DISCUSSIONS

This chapter presents the results of interview conducted among the LGUs in Maguindanao, including the regional, provincial, and municipal members of the executive, legislative and administrative branches, members of the negotiating panels - both from the government and the MILF -and a representative from the Office of the Presidential Adviser on the Peace Process. It also focuses on their involvement, particularly narrating their experiences and some challenges encountered in leveraging their assertions for greater access, as well as in mobilizing their legitimate representations in the process.

Participants' Profile

The participants were composed of 4 groups — BTC commissioners, OPAPP, Local Government Units, and officials from the provincial and regional government. Except for the two (2) BTC representatives and an official of OPAPP, all participants were from the mainland province — Maguindanao — of ARMM. These participants were carefully selected based on their participation, involvement and official designation relating to the Mindanao peace process.

A total of 38 representatives among the 4 groups have participated in the key informant interviews and focus group discussion with 82% are from LGU, 10% are from the provincial and regional governments, and the remaining 8% came from the BTC and OPAPP. Classified by the two branches of government — executive and legislative — 68% (24 participants) are officials under the executive branch while, 32% (11 participants) are from the legislative branch (this is based on the total number of officials - 35 representatives - from the local, provincial and regional government units). Their mean age was 46 years old. Eighty percent (80%) were males and 20% were females.

TABLE 2   Selected Characteristics of the Participants

Selected Characteristics		LGU	Regional and Provincial Gov't	Total
		(82%)	(8%)	(90%)
1) Branch of Gov't	No. in the Executive	22 (62%)	2 (6%)	24 (68%)
	No. in the Legislative	9 (26%)	2 (6%)	11 (32%)
2) Mean Age (in years)		42	49	46
3) Sex	No. of Male	26 (74%)	2 (6%)	28 (80%)
	No. of Female	5 (24%)	2 (6%)	7 (20%)

LGUs involvement in the GPH-MILF peace process

Maguindanao LGU Perspectives

Based on the OPAPP 2015 data, of the total 553 consultations in the whole of ARMM, there were 100 consultations undertaken specifically for LGUs. The figure amounts to a mere 18% LGU consultations. Comparably, the larger 453 consultations were conducted solely as multi-sectoral consultations. Moving down to the Maguindanao scenario, the same pattern of numerical discrepancy is manifested. Of the total 44, only 8 consultations were undertaken for LGUs and 36 were for the multi-sector.[4] Specifically, Maguindanao LGUs were engaged in only two (2) consultations back in 2010-2011, three (3) in 2012-2013, and three (3) in 2014-2015. Overall, there is a big discrepancy in the number of consultations done for LGUs.

Moreover, the minimal consultations were actually information dissemination on what's happening in the peace process, as well as, on the content of the proposed law; rather than the needed exchange of opinions, discussions on the provisions, and trade-off of proposals between and among the LGUs and the negotiating panels. Added to that, the articulated counter proposals of

---
[4]   Projection based on the OPAPP 2015 data.

LGUs were not seriously taken into considerations and reflected in the text of the draft basic law. When taken as a whole, the data would show a very weak nature and character of LGU involvement and participation in the consultation process undertaken in the whole broader peace process.

Some LGUs saw the lack of political representation of their sector in the formal negotiations. Admittedly, they believe that there were only few consultations specifically designed for LGUs that have been organized by the negotiating panels. One LGU official lamented thus:

> "Sa totoo lang po talaga, isa yan sa mga hinanaing ng ating LGU. Yun bang meron tayong lack of political participation sa proseso. However, despite the fact na hindi tayo nata-tap, ang LGU ay ginagawa ang lahat para iboluntaryo ang sarili na magsagawa ng mga activities sa probinsya na may koneksyon sa peace process"
>
> *(To be honest, one of the complaint and resentment of the LGU is our lack of political participation in the process. However, despite the fact that we were not tap, we in LGU are voluntarily doing our initiatives to facilitate activities in the province related to the peace process.)*

Furthermore, LGUs' acknowledged the significance of inclusivity for the peace process to move forward effectively, and they believe that the LGU as a structure should also be recognized and invited in forums or consultations that would let them raise their concerns and/or issues that they think would matter in the lives of their constituents. Although, they have been invited by the negotiating panels/OPAPP into different consultation activities, they are certain that most of the information disseminating and knowledge based fora were spearheaded by the different civil society groups, wherein different agendas on the Mindanao peace process were presented and discussed. As expounded by one of the officials from the first district:

> "Para po natin ma-achieve yung peace and development sa Mindanao, dapat inclusive po yung pag-imbita, na kung saan lahat po ng sector ay may representation pati na din po ang LGU. Ang mga NGOs nandyan sila para tulungan kami, sila yung nag- uupdate sa amin ng mga pangyayari sa peace agenda sa Mindanao. Sila yung nagsisilbi naming "backbone" sa pagbuo ng pundasyon at kaalam tungkol dito"
>
> *(To achieve peace and development in Mindanao, the invitation in the process should be inclusive, wherein there are actual representations from the LGU and other sectors. NGOs had been helping us in gaining and increasing our*

knowledge on the current peace and development agenda in Mindanao, they have been our backbone in creating a foundation of knowledge in the discourse.)

Conversely, two (2) LGU participants attested that they were equally represented in the negotiating table, since it is a negotiation led by the government between the moro fronts, in particular, the LGUs have realized their representation through the government's stand and positions on the process. In which, directives and representation from the national administration is an equal participation of the LGU in the Bangsamoro peace agenda to take its course, as such, one of the officials from the second district argued that:

> "Kami sa LGU ay talaga namang well represented sa pamamagitan ng government negotiating panel, since we are working in the government, naniniwala po kami na ang national administration is doing everything para po masama ang aming mga posisyon at artikulasyon dito sa future Bangsamoro Government."

> *(We in the LGU are actually well represented through the government negotiting panel, since we are working in the government, we believe that the national administration is doing everything to include our positions and articulations in the future Bangsamoro government.)*

Aside from that, some LGUs, in particular, who are closely associated with the MILF sought after the significance of bringing down the negotiating panel to the community to be able to listen and talk with the people, in particular, different representatives and sectors in the locality, on matters pertaining to the issues and concerns they saw in the small and bigger picture of creating a new law that would answer the Bangsamoro problem on gaining autonomy, and exercising their right to self-determination. Thus, these collaborative initiatives were undertaken to broaden the arena for political dialogue and creating more spaces and platform for an extensive and meaningful consultations to ensure that the BBL or any law that will be submitted to Congress is practically more inclusive and more substantive as a legislative document. In fact, these LGU officials are reaching those who are formally engaged on the negotiations and express their gesture of support and manifestations in voluntarily participating in any related activities of the process — and to be able to show their sincerity, LGU officials, specifically, the Governor and other local chief executives (mayors) are willingly invites themselves to any formal meetings and national or regional occasions celebrating by the negotiating team in support to the current peace process.

"Ang ating pong Governor ay nagkukusang makisali sa kahit anong diskusyon, formal gatherings, consultations at okasyon sa ating bansa o sa labas man. Ito po ay isang gesture of support ng ating Governor to express yung supporta ng probinsya sa nangyayaring negosasyon. Ito din yung aming natatanging paraan, para makapagpahayag ng aming mga posisyon at articulation dito sa magiging bagong gobyerno para sa Bangsamoro."

(*Our Governor is submissively engaging in any platform or discussions, formal gatherings, consultations and occasions in our country or outside — this is one gesture of the governor to express the province support to the ongoing peace negotiations. In which, it is a way where we can ventilate our positions and articulations in the future Bangsamoro Government*)

Principally, local, international and national civil society organizations and government links and agencies that mobilize widespread support and bring together the political entity of the Bangsamoro imparted additional weight to LGUs' voices in the peace process. Actions may include: regional wide and local wide peace walks and writing public letters and submission of position papers to the government; or media campaigns and informal campaigns through conferences, consultation meetings and forums — mostly used platform to tackle their sentiments, apprehensions and concerns in the process.

Nevertheless, the view of the LGU in their involvement in the peace process is heterogeneous. There are four (4) points and narratives that came out during the interview: (1) LGUs are not well represented and consulted in the peace process, since few consultations were spearheaded for their sector; (2) some believe they are equally represented through the government negotiating panel, in which, it is a government led process; (3) LGUs association and links with the MILF and/or negotiating panel had helped them gain access to the consultations and peace negotiation; and (4) LGUs have been mostly consulted and involved by the local CSOs — through invitation or partnership.

However, most of them understand that despite their critical contributions to security, their representation in peace processes has lagged. Continued failure to include the political entity in peace processes ignores their demonstrated effectiveness and overlooks a potential strategy to respond effectively to security threats in the locality, as well as in the country. As such, for them it is crucial to **recognize and augment national institutional mechanisms and 'homes' for the local government units' participation and involvement**.

Generally speaking, the involvement of the LGUs in the whole Bangsamoro peace process is complex — from formal consultations, participation through linkages and alliances, and voluntarily creating platforms for dialogues. However, these are indirect and weak forms of participation. If at all, Local Government Units' issues and articulations have become mere consideration during the on-going peace negotiations due to three aspects: (1) The shift in longing for the peace process to be all inclusive, transparent, and accountable from 2012 — signing of FAB and CAB, and up until now with the direct mandate from the President; (2) An argument resulting over the Regional-LGU relations in the Bangsamoro Law, that enable the need for the LGUs to participate; and (3) The unremitting leveraging of the common apprehensions and articulations of some local political leaders during consultation activities. There is informal alliance recognized and acknowledged by the LGUs as their coordination mechanisms in support to the peace process. Moreover, they believe that they were able to create their own platform orspace that would address their localities specific needs and suitable alternative solutions and interventions in the common issues in the municipality.

From the Bangsamoro Transition Commission perspective

There was no formal mechanism to ensure the representation and participation of LGUs in the Mindanao peace negotiations, and, as a result, LGUs were neither formally represented nor participated in the peace talks in the earlier stage of the process. One of the Commissioner of the Bangsamoro Transition Commission admittedly express that some LGUs have not been accessed, but at some point, there are representatives from the LGUs that have been appropriately consulted from the time of the negotiations, to the time of the drafting of the Bangsamoro law, and the hearings of the committee in the last House Bill 4994. Additionally, in the current negotiation, the House of Representatives will still conduct mandatory consultations in the Bangsamoro core territory, and will engage the local government unit - as the Commissioner guarantees:

> "… now there would still be consultations, I was told by the congress, that they will be conducting seven (7) mandatory consultations in the area, and it will engage the local government unit … therefore the articulations of the local government can already be put in."

To date back, in 2015, during the public hearings conducted by the former Senator Ferdinand Marcos Jr. of the Senate on local government committee, he revealed that there is an issue of exclusion of various stakeholders during the process of drafting the proposed BBL — in particular, a former Congressman/Mayor of Jolo, Sulu assumed that the BBL is a one-sided bill that favors the Moro Islamic Liberation Front because other sectors were not consulted about it (Santos, 2015). The former Congressman/Mayor have said that the local governments in the core territory of the proposed Bangsamoro political entity were left out of consultations. Pointing out the composition of the first Bangsamoro Transition Commission team, the official expressed:

> "Sad to say, the power has been given to the MILF... it appears to be all MILF, none from other sectors."

Although, the issue of inclusivity is being questioned during the first proposed BBL, nevertheless, LGUs started to gain direct access to the negotiations as the political space began to open incrementally during the composition of the new expanded Bangsamoro Transition Commission wherein the regional and local government were represented by two Commissioners in the present expanded BTC.

Consequently, the appointment of Commissioner B were never a representation of the LGU, since the official was then nominated by a friend who have direct links in the Malacañang. As the commissioner explained during the interview:

> "I was not actually directly nominated to represent the LGU, consequently, I was in Malacañang with a friend. It was at the same time, one spot were not been fill in, and it was automatically given to me, through recommendation."

Even though the appointment of Commissioner B was not directly to represent the LGU, the official specified that through his experiences as local chief executive and a former member of the lower house, he was able to help in the articulation the common sentiments of the LGU in the old draft of the BBL. One of the provisions he clearly saw and examined in the Framework Agreement on the Bangsamoro (FAB) and its four annexes is the non- diminution of LGU privileges already granted to the LGU under the current ARMM setup. The typescript in the FAB on non-diminution delivers:

> "The privileges already enjoyed by the local government units under existing laws shall not be diminished unless otherwise altered, modified or reformed for good governance pursuant to the provisions of the Bangsamoro local government code."

This non-diminution principle, Commissioner B asserted, comes with the admonition of good governance, from now the circumstances under which any of the privileges can be "altered, modified or reformed" to serve good governance should be elucidated in the Basic Law. He is certain that this and additional privileges can be provided in the Basic Law to attract inclusion of more LGUs in the Bangsamoro. However, he then acknowledged that the documents — the FAB and the four annexes — are not absolutely understood in the LGUs' circle, something that the two parties, the GPH and MILF, should deal with the level expectations.

Commissioner B also emphasized that the presence of political leaders at any consultation activities should be considered. The Bangsamoro, the negotiating panel and the government, should institutionalize inclusivity and representations of each sectors in the development in the region. It must create and implement policies addressing the vulnerability of these sectors. Participation of every individual and sector in governance and nation- building must be upheld, he added.

Nevertheless, through the representations of the two commissioners in the expanded BTC, they were able to articulate the positions of the regional and local government units in the current proposed Bangsamoro law — as an assurance, Commissioner A pointed out that:

> "…although, there are no representatives from the local government units in the negotiating panel, LGUs' have been well represented in the BTC, wherein their common sentiments and positions were also been carried out meaningfully in the submitted proposed legislative document for the Bangsamoro."

In summary, the representation of the LGUs, for the BTC, have been sought through the two appointed Commissioners. Nevertheless, collective positions and articulations of the LGU -from the previous consultations until before drafting the new law - were carried out meaningfully in the proposed legislative document that would create a new Bangsamoro government.

Consequently, there are four (4) facets of involvement that came out during the interview with the Local Government Units in Maguindanao, these reasons have different angle and complexities. These facets of involvements have link to the different experiences attaching the LGUs personal designation, association and support to the process, as such, these participation have been defined in a more crucial way. For example, political leaders, in particular, the local chief executives and the governor are being directly tapped by the negotiating panel without proper channeling the invitation in their respective LGUs, since then, technical people — mostly, administrative officers and designated officials have never sought the engagement to be either a direct consultation or just a matter of personal linkage or association. However, there are some local chief executives/officials that have expressed that the LGUs political participation remains nascent — although there were no direct involvement for them, this groups maintained their support by activating their facilitative roles through creating a platform or joining any consultation activities to express their unrelenting support to the process. Another classic example that was raised in the interview, is the participation of the LGUs through invitations and partnerships with the Civil Society Organizations in the conduct of forums, conferences and consultation meetings in their locality and/or any avenues to raised their specific concerns in the process — this kind of participation falls back also to their roles as a political leader/manager whose working behind the negotiating panel or the process itself. As a result, these instances make up the definition of an "indirect participation" through back channeling their support in any diverse form of actions to mobilize and prevent the stagnancy of the peace process to move forward.

Nevertheless, to counter the observation of the LGUs on their representation, one of the BTC commissioner expressed that the common articulations and the sentiments of the sector on the proposed Bangsamoro government have been included and crafted meaningfully in the new 2017 proposed draft Bangsamoro law. This in any way was supported and backed-up by a former member of the House of Representatives, and a former mayor of a municipality in ARMM, in particular, the Municipality of Jolo in the Province of Sulu. The BTC member that in a leeway helped the BTC commissioners to comprehend and shaped the LGUs agenda is Commissioner Hussin Amin — he specifically addressed the non-diminution principle in the FAB wherein the "privileges already enjoyed by the local government units" under the existing laws and provisions in the ARMM and/or national government "shall not be diminished unless otherwise altered, modified or reformed for good governance" in pursuant to the provisions of Local Government Code that will be created in the future Bangsamoro government. As to compare, Article VI, Sec 7, in the new basic law crafted the Intergovernmental relations between the Bangsamorro Regional government and the LGU stated that:

> "... The authority to regulate on its own responsibility the affairs of the local government units is guaranteed within the limit of this Basic Law. The Local

Government Units shall continue to exercise the powers granted to them as provided by law. For good governance, the Bangsamoro Parliament may enact a Local Government Code." (pp. 22)

Needless to say, the new crafted Bangsamoro law assurances the local government units that there will be no diminutions on the powers and functions as well as the privileges that are long-drawn-out to them by the present laws such as the Local Government Code of 1991 or the RA 7160.

Experiences and Challenges in the Peace Process

Both the negotiating panel agenda and the "LGU's agenda" were shaped through open facilitated dialogues with a diverse range of local government unit constituents — they had shaped their agendas through their experiences and challenges faced in the process, thus it helped them realize their significant role in keeping the process to move forward.

Undeniably, during the start of the consultation in 2010, local political leaders view the peace process through narrow lens of parochial and partisan interests where the BBL and normalization and decommissioning processes are threats to their hold to political power.

Local Government Units (specifically, the local chief executives) are mainly focused on whether under the Bangsamoro law, they are able to preserve their political powers, or not. However, through unremitting engagement in the Bangsamoro discourse and ongoing consultations, stressing "autonomy" vis a vis BBL steered and raised their level of engagement from discussion to political dialogue among other who are pushing for inclusivity and understanding on setting up a new regional government for Bangsamoro.

> "Dati naman talaga, hindi namin alam kung kailangan ba talaga ay kasama kami sa proseso. Honestly, nakita namin na medyo hindi inclusive yung proseso. Nakita din namin na maaring maging threat ito sa aming current role as elected officials sa LGU. Marami kaming mga assumptions at confusions sa dating proseso, hindi naming maintindihan kung ano ba talaga yung magiging epekto nito sa amin. However, nang dahil na din siguro sa aming curiosity at willingness na makibahagi sa proseso ng Bangsamoro, nagkaroon kami ng mas malinaw na pananaw at kasagutan sa mga common na questions na parati naming tinatanong."
>
> (*Since before, we don't know if we are needed to be part of the process. Honestly, we saw that the process is not that inclusive. We also saw that this can be a threat*

to our current role as elected officials in the LGU. We have a lot of assumptions and confusions to the old process, we do not understand what will be the effect of this process to us. However, with our curiosity and willingness to be part of the Bangsamoro process, our common questions were clearly answered.)

Through dialogues, they were able to understand that their political interests is better served by a strong autonomous institution where LGUs are an integral part, thus, they have realize that the level of local autonomy they aspire for, is promising under a strong regional autonomous arrangement. As a result, they began to explore that local autonomy is achievable if they participate, support, and sustain the discussion on the evolving concept of autonomy within the broader peace process.

> "Nung naintindihan na namin yung napapaloob at hangarin ng pagbuo ng Bangsamoro Basic Law ay mas nakita namin ang malaking pagkakataon na mas mapanatili o mapalawak yung "autonomy" na hinahangad ng mga LGU. Higit sa lahat, mas naunawaan namin na mas nakakabuti at advantage para sa amin, sa LGU, na maging involve sa usapin ng Bangsamoro peace process, hindi lamang sa negotiation kundi pati na rin sa pagbuo ng isang gobyerno para sa Bangsamoro"

> *(When we already understand what's inside the Bangsamoro Basic Law and its goal, we saw the chance to maintain and expand the envisioned "autonomy" of LGU. More so than that, we also realize that it would be better and more advantage for us, in LGU, to be involved in the Bangsamoro peace discourse, not only in the negotiation but also in the creation of the Bangsamoro government.)*

The LGUs and local political leaders seized any forums, FGDs, and RTDs that were planned and conducted by different agencies from the government and international and local based organizations, since this has been their long-awaited window of opportunity to engage with the negotiating panels, senate, congress, OPAPP, security cluster of the executive branch, and the international organizations on issues pertinent to local governance and security anchored in the proposed Bangsamoro law. This was evidently expressed in their persistence to co-organize with CSOs to conduct and initiate any follow-up consultation workshops and forums where they could further ventilate their sentiments on the issues and also present their corresponding suggestions and proposals. As officials from the first district have positioned:

> "Ginagawa naman naming lahat para ma-reach out namin ang negotiating panel regarding on our sentiments and positions in the establishment of

the Bangsamoro Government, that is why kami ay tumutulong sa pag-organize ng forums, workshops, at pati na rin sa pagimbita ng membryo ng negotiating team, in particular with the MILF to attend and explain further yung consensus points in the proposed law, para na din maintindihan ng LGU kung ano ang napapaloob sa Bangsamoro Basic Law"

(We are doing everything to reach out with the negotiating panel regarding our sentiments and positions in the establishment of a Bangsamoro Government, that is why we are helping in the organizing of forums, workshops and request any member of the negotiating team, in particular with the MILF, to attend and explain further the consensus points in the proposed law, so that the LGUs will be able to understand what is inside the Bangsamoro Basic Law.)

The LGUs are holding their hope to the forthcoming legislation for the Bangsamoro, saying that the Basic Law must be able to deliver real autonomy this time around, thus, they share the view that autonomy in the ARMM is partly a failure because of incomplete devolution of powers, as one of the participants have believed:

"Ang pinaka main problem ng ARMM ay yung kanyang structure at yung incomplete devolution of powers"

(The main problem of the ARMM is its structure and the incomplete implementation of the devolution of powers.)

The problem in the structure twigs from issues and concerns on the powers established from the national government to the regional government down to the local government units (LGUs) — as such, this problem is compounded by incomplete devolution. In ARMM devolution, powers from the national government to the regional government were not been completed and the powers from the regional government to the LGUs, specifically, at the provincial level were not been fully downloaded (IAG, 2014).

Whatever the case, LGUs highlighted that it is imperative to visualize the Bangsamoro in relations of how the devolution should ensue. Instead of be dependent on executive orders and any conflicting laws of devolution available, the Bangsamoro Law may arrange for a "wholesale" devolution — in which, it is one of the drivers of the participation and involvement of the LGUs in any consultation activities.

Consequently, for LGUs, their experiences in informal peace processes — related to their mandates as leaders in the locality - are vastly significant for official peace processes and peace negotiations. Even when they think that they were being denied to access to formal structures, they can contribute their experience as 'change agents' in informal peace processes and local peace activism in their locality. As such, they have observed that the peace process have largely contributed in the maintenance of the peace and order in the locality, since, there is an ongoing process, there are programs being implemented under the CAB that is effective in the ground — for instance, the existing mechanisms for ceasefire and normalization — had helped prevented and/or lessen conflicts that is happening in the locality. As added by one of the executives in the second district:

> "… nang dahil po sa peace process, natulungan nito na ma-maintain ng lokalidad ang kanilang peace and order. Aside from that, kami po sa LGU ay nagagawa po naming mabigay at ma-deliver yung mga basic services ng aming komunidad ng walang kaguluhan. Mas konti yung conflict, mas nagkakaroon ng maraming oportunidad para sa Bangsamoro na makamit ang isang makabuluhang buhay"
>
> (*Because of the peace process, it helped the locality in maintaining its peace and order. Aside from that, we in the LGU, can deliver peacefully the basic services needed by our constituents. Less conflict means more opportunity for the Bangsamoro to have a meaningful life.*)

Ultimately, however, peace was a narrowly participatory process for LGU's. Their goals and aspirations for the peace agreements were resulting from a desire to overcome the difficult realities faced by the Bangsamoro, including women, youth, and elderly, and among others in participatory governance and nation building. Bringing an end to the struggle and moving past violence was the adhesive that bound the political leaders together and worked as the flagship of their platform for change. The change that they are pushing through will effectively happen if they will be more platforms and avenues exclusively for the LGU to say their piece, however, they also see the significant of their alternative mechanisms and solutions for their voices to be heard — this includes joining into RTDs, FGDs and any window of opportunity to be in the platform where voices are being heard by the negotiating panel. Thus, as shared by one of the officials from the second district:

> "Sa tingin ko po, kailangan po ng Bangsamoro na magkaroon ng sariling gobyerno. Nakita po natin yung struggle ng ating kapwa Bangsamoro sa pagsulong ng aming "right to self-determination", hindi lamang po diyan

nagtatapos kundi pa na rin sa mga karanasan ng ating kababaihan, kabataan, at ating mga kababayan na naghahangad na makibahagi sa pamumuno. In addition, sabihin man natin na naging exclusive lamang yung usapin at negosasyon sa bagay na ito, ngunit sa tingin ko, nakita namin sa LGU na kailangan naming makisabay at makisali para na din makamit natin yung tunay na pagbabago sa gobyerno."

(In my personal opinion, the Bangsamoro (people) needs to have their own government. We saw the struggle of our Bangsamoro (people) to push for our right to self-determination, and it doesn't just end there, the experiences of our women, youth and the Bangsamoro people who wanted to be part of the governance are being sought. In addition, though the negotiation have been exclusive, however, for the LGU, we saw the need to participate in the process to be able to achieve a real change in the government.)

Consequently, one of the officials have brought up the challenge on participating to the gatherings and consultations, since most of the events and activities where organized and held in a capital city or in province wherein there participation and attendance is not lagged. Practically speaking, they saw this as a big gap of access of the people/community in the negotiating panels — thus, making it more exclusive to those people who can have the access. As further added by the official:

"Isa ding nakikita naming gap ay yung pagsagawa mismo ng mga consultations, events and meetings sa mga big city or capital city, pwede din nating sabihin sa sentro lamang. Mahirap kasi kaming nasa LGU pati na rin yung nasa komunidad ay gusto naming makisali at masabi kung ano yung nais naming iparating sa kanila. Ngunit dahil na din hindi nila nadadala at the local level yung usapin at consultation, nanghihinyang kami na hindi maisali or kahit man lang mapakinggan kung ano yung aming pagtingin dito sa buong proseso at pagtingin na din sa pagbuo ng future Bangsamoro government. Sayang lang, sana may mga konsultasyon na grounded sa locality at mapakinggan kami lahat."

(One of the gaps that we saw during the consultations, meetings and events is it was organized in the capital city or big city, or we can just say, it was mostly held in the center places. It was hard for us since the community and the LGU wanted to take part in and say our piece to them, however, due to the lack of bringing the consultation at the local level, unfortunately our positions and articulations on the way we look at in the whole process, and the establishment

of the Bangsamoro government were not being heard. We hope that we have consultations that is grounded in the locality to be able to hear everyone.)

While the central government acknowledged the legitimate demand for expression of identity of the MILF, it also had to cogitate that there are other sectors consist of almost half of the population of the area which respectively need preservation of their identity and their rights. The forbidding challenge then was permitting acceptable expressions of diversity during actual consultations and dialogues.

Mostly though, the consultations and dialogues are only limited to the awareness and added information on the process — consultation and hearing activities to share their stands and viewpoints were not properly addressed since the meetings is practically focused on the local peace and security concerns and other related agenda. Limited consultation, absence of LGU entity in the BTC, and the non-inclusion of LGU voice in the draft basic law, all add-up to the belief that LGUs were not given the space to substantively participate in the peace process. The hard part is, they will be the ones later who will play the major role in implementing whatever will be finally agreed. If they could not find their interest in the agreement; the whole implementation process would be greatly jeopardized.

Generally speaking, the LGUs understanding on the establishment of the Bangsamoro government is optimistic, however, at the same time, they are dejected that the negotiating panels should have closely reach out to them and consulted by necessitating their representation in the negotiating table. Nonetheless, the feeling of being sidelined is not rumbling into tangible discontent.

Inter-LGU Coordination Mechanisms

There are 2 ways by which Local Government Units pull their political capitals and resources to leverage their participation in the peace process. These are: inter-LGU alliances, and the Provincial Peace and Order Council. The first is an LGU-initiated local formation, while the second is nationally-mandated special body lodged at the provincial level.

Majority of local government unit officials used their personal and professional networks to mobilize individuals and alliances, as well as organize activities. For example, municipalities in the Province of Maguindanao formed alliances and/or inter-LGU coordination mechanisms to create a fluid network in their respective legislative districts, in order to coordinate and monitor specific agendas that will shape a conducive political environment —thus creating space towards a consensus on the commitment and programs that greatly benefit their allied localities. Pertinent issues on local peace and security, and peace and development are always the major items in the agenda during regular meetings of the alliance, where the current peace roadmap and/or updates on the GPH-MILF peace process is thoroughly discussed and analyzed.

Although these alliances were formed and initiated by the Philippine Army, in particular, Brigade Commanders on the ground, robust support and commitment from the local chief executives became the main engines behind the establishment and sustainability of the alliance, which are working up until now. For instance, the Iranun Inter-Agency Task Force — composed of the municipalities of Barira, Buldon, Matanog and Parang. Then there is also the Nuling Inter-Agency Alliance which is constituted of the following municipalities

Sultan Kudarat and Sultan Mastura. Both alliances focus on the holistic aspect of governance, peace and security development, especially issues of peace and order situation in their own localities. Among these, hard issues in the GPH-MILF peace process are seriously tackled, as most of their constituents rely on updates and information from their local heads and officials. One local official explained:

> "... though the alliance is not specifically mandated for the peace process, we make use of the platform para pag-usapan naming yung mga walang sawa naming pagsuporta sa proseso dahil naniniwala kami na itong aming maliit na alliance ay para bagang aming small advocacy at para matulungan ating mga negotiators to move the process. Higit pa po diyan, nagiging space na din namin ito sa pamamagitan ng small gatherings at meeting para mapag-usapan namin ang mga tunay na nangyayari sa peace process at pati na rin sa local and security ng Bangsamoro as a whole."

> *(Though the alliance is not specifically mandated for the peace process, we make use of the platform to talk about our unrelenting support to the process because we believe that the alliance can be a form of small advocacy and help the negotiators to move the process. Moreover, small gatherings and meetings of our alliance became our space to talk about the realities of the peace process and also the local and security of the Bangsamoro as a whole.)*

On the southern part of the province, Task Force "Kapamagayun" (Unity) is also exerting the same effort to strengthen the governance aspect in the allied localities, which comprises the municipalities of Northern Kabuntalan, Datu Odin Sinsuat, Guindulungan, Talayan, Datu Anggal Midtimbang and Talitay. Deliberations and discussions of their peace and security issues include threat to terrorism, and illegal drugs. In general, the topic on peace process have been sidelined in the discussions and meetings of the member LGUs in the task force, as clarified by one of the officials who have been part of the alliance have said:

> "Ang Task Force Kapamagayun ay binuo para suportahan ng mga LGUs ang isa't isa para sa peace and development agenda ng kanilang lokalidad. Yung mga local security issues ay naa-address ditto, pati na rin yung pag-keep track sa nangyayaring negosasyon ay napag-uusapan sa diskusyon kasama ang mga mayors at security officials."
>
> (*Task Force Kapamagayun is created to support each LGU in their peace and development agenda in their own locality. Local security have been addressed, thus, keeping track on the negotiations were also laid down in our discussions with other mayors and security officials.*)

Furthermore, LGUs recognize the Provincial Peace and Order Council (PPOC) as one of the established inter-LGU coordination mechanisms that is in existence. The PPOC is pursuant to the Local Government Code (LGC) of 1991 which mandates of the provinces to operationalize and create a committee which formulates and adopts effective mechanisms for the coordination, cooperation, and consultation involving the local executives, citizenry and law enforcement agencies. Further, the council plans, monitors, and implements provisions and programs suited to the needs of their localities. Regular discussions include the topics of livelihood, social and economic wellbeing of the area, and most importantly the current local peace and order situation. Moreover, the council is also convened to address immediate peace and order, and public safety. Particular to the Bangsamoro areas, common articulations and negotiations on the Bangsamoro Basic Law (BBL) and the broader peace process are usually included in the discussions. However, these are in the form of awareness raising and information dissemination. Indeed, some questions pertaining to especially power-sharing were raised together with some recommendations. But the LGUs could not find their recommendations incorporated in the final draft. Hence they could not find the LGU voice in the draft basic law in particular.

> "Nakikita ko na isa naming coordination mechanism between and among LGUs ay yung quarterly meeting na pinapatawag ng ating Governor sa buong probinsya ng Maguindanao. Ito ay tinatawag na Provincial Peace and Order Council (PPOC), isa itong mandato ng gobyerno para pag-usapan at talakayin ang security situations ng lugar. Bagamat isa itong meeting at pagpupulong para sa security issues at ibang development issues, hindi namin nakakalimutan na maisali din sa usapin yung patungkol sa peace process, sa nagaganap na pag-uusap ng gobyerno at ng MILF sa pagbuo ng bagong Bangsamoro Government."

> *(The quarterly meeting that is organize by the Governor between and among the LGUs in the province have been sought to be a form of a coordination mechanism. It is called as the Provincial Peace and Order Council (PPOC), a mandate from the government to tackle issues of security situations in the area. Although, it is intended to be a gathering on the discussion of security issues and other development issues, we never forget to include the topics of the peace process, and the current negotiation between the MILF and the government in the establishment of a new Bangsamoro Government.)*

Basically, they formed and joined alliances with other sectors to realize unfamiliar themes, relied on CSOs who understand and respect their political interests. In the case of Maguindanao, LGUs relied on their voluntary partnership with the Institute for Autonomy and Governance (IAG) to forward their voices to the government and the rebel groups especially during the crafting of the Bangsamoro Basic Law. Sulu LGUs in particular, sought the assistance of IAG to directly communicate their queries and proposals on the BBL to the Senate, the Lower House, as well as to the MILF. The same nature of LGU — CSO alliances exist in ZamBaSulTa[5] area, where the Zamboanga Basilan Integrated Alliance (a local NGO) facilitates LGU dialogues with the peace process actors. Over time, a collaborative spirit nurtured between the LGUs and representatives of many other sectors, particularly those who have recognized their apprehensions, and facilitated them to realize their significant role in the Bangsamoro.

> "We also sought the formation of coordination or pwede na ding alliance with local CSOs, and other institutions para facilitate yung aming positions at articulations sa establishment ng Bangsamoro government, nandyan ang IAG para suportahan kami at bigyan ng kaalaman sa mga nangyayari sa

---

[5] ZamBaSulTa refers to the whole geo-political and economic zone covering Zamboanga, Basilan, Sulu, and Tawitawi area.

negosasyon. Hindi din namin maitatanggi na naging malaking bahagi sila sa facilitation ng aming hinaing at apprehensions sa nangyayaring usapin."

(We also sought the formation of coordination or alliance with local CSOs, and other institutions to facilitate our positions and articulations in the establishment of the Bangsamoro government — IAG is there who supports us by giving updates and knowledge on the current negotiation. We cannot deny the fact that they were a big help in the facilitation of our resentment and apprehensions on the ongoing negotiations.)

Although, it has been clearly stated that the aforementioned alliances and coordination mechanisms are not solely dedicated to the peace process agenda — LGU have used this links to keep themselves to be well-informed, and to express their support in the peace process. Consequently, for others, they have leveraged personal relationships with representatives of other sectors whom they knew prior to the crafting of the Bangsamoro law and they also conducted strategic outreach to make new connections. The political sector had relied on convergence in similar social identities and interests, creating common ground based on shared values, beliefs and positions. For instance, parts of the political entity collaborated with the local CSOs to ensure the issue of the local government was reflected in the proposal, and other parts maintained their relationships with individuals in the negotiating panel, in particular, in the MILF.

The participation or direct involvement of the LGUs in the peace process have been differently defined in a manner of perceptions between those who have been engaged vis a vis to those who have been left out. Like in any other consultations, there will be individuals who will not be involved, however, their sector as a group, through representations have been consulted — points to consider in these facets of participation have drawn out to the (a) possibility of consulting wide-range of individuals versus sectoral representatives, and (b) accessibility of the individual or sectoral groups to the actors involved in the consultation. The first describe for a vague positions to be consider based on individuality and not as a group — in this cases, sectoral representatives have been more sought than to involved a larger audience for consultations, in order to cope up with the deadlines and craft a specified narrative of issues and concerns, whereas the latter is compounded to the problem of opportunity versus accessibility — opportunity is the chance to be involved but it never guarantees the accessibility to the common or people who does not have direct associations or link to the table, while accessibility have both the opportunity and the direct contact to the persons in the negotiating table.

Nonetheless, LGUs relied on new alliances — especially with NGOs - in order to help negotiate their political interests in the peace process. They also relied on support from other sectors with shared goals to leverage their positions.

Dominant Assertions on the need for LGUs' political participation

LGUs believe that they play a variety of roles in multifaceted, multitrack peace processes. They can sit at the formal negotiating table, on a technical working group or sub commission, or they can be exterior the talks involved as political leaders representing the LGUs in following development agendas, thus, all of these roles are critical. In the current process, political actors assumed they played a key role in their local mobilization and in articulating their difficulties and concerns. These relentless voices played a vital role in fortifying a number of provisions for LGUs in the final agreements. As one of the executives of the first district have said:

> "Marami na kaming nagawang mga paraan to reach and access the committee or commission involved sa pagsagawa ng draft legislative document for the Bangsamoro. We strongly believe, bilang leaders ng aming lokalidad, we can do more and articulate our positions for the benefit of our constituents."
>
> (We have grasped countless of methodologies to reach and access the committee/commission involved in the drafting of a legislative document for the Bangsamoro. We strongly believe, that as the leaders in the locality, we can do more and articulate our positions for the benefit of our constituents.)

There is an inclination to view "LGUs' issues" in moderately a narrow way. It is imperative to break out of this narrow understanding—so that a "wholesale package" for good governance, right provision for basic services for the Bangsamoro and manageable peace and security situation can be achieved. For example, LGUs have been in the forefront of delivering basic services and implying good governance in their own locality — they have been elected and trusted by the people — so common understanding and realities in the ground are mostly addressed by these political leaders, as a result, LGUs have been aiming for an inclusion and understanding of their role in the crafting of a new Bangsamoro Government in order to improve and enhance the LGU structure and mechanisms in delivering basic services to the locality. To prove this, one of the members of the Sangguniang Bayan in the second district have explained that:

> "… meron pong significant role na dapat ang LGU ay ma-recognize sa peace process. Basically, the locality look up to their elected officials — nakikinig sila, sumusunog at nirerespeto nito ang kanilang mga leaders. If in any case, maramdaman ng ating mamamayan na ang kanilang mga elected officials ay being neglected sa proseso na ito, they might not trust the process. Ito lamang po ay assumption, sapagkat nakikita natin na malaki yung tiwala ng taong bayan sa kanilang mga leaders. Ang pag-elect nila dito ay isang gesture na hinahayaan nila ang kanilang leader na magpasya para sa ikakabuti ng lahat."

> *(There is a significant role that the LGUs should be recognized in the peace process. Basically, the locality looks up to their elected officials — they listened, they follow and respected their leaders. If in any case, the people will feel that their elected officials are being neglected in the process, they might not trust the process. This is only an assumption since the community has the high trust to their leaders — their election to the position is one of the gesture that the people are entrusting the decision for the betterment of everyone to their leaders.)*

Furthermore, for political actors and other broad range of Bangsamoro groups be able to engage in the process, and to ensure a broad base of participation, mechanisms must be established for sectoral consultation processes. Collectively, LGUs agree that each of the sector have its own role in the process, and for the legislative document for the Bangsamoro to be realized meaningfully, sectoral representations and consultations should have been observed

One of the officials asserted that whatever the case of the current negotiation is, whether they have been tapped nor engaged with, the LGUs will remain to be the face of the locality in any engagements that would leverage the needs and benefits of the community in the national and regional peace discourse. Although he was then disappointed with the fast tracking of consultations happened in the current proposed BBL, he was then gladly expecting that through the ongoing public hearings and consultations by the lower and upper houses, sentiments and common issues on the LGU-Regional relations must be address, for that the complete devolution of powers and authentic autonomy should be realized in the future Bangsamoro Government. According to him:

"... the authenticity of autonomy that the government promised to the Bangsamoro people should have been included in the proposed Bangsamoro law. In which, ang LGU ay magampanan nila yung Local Government Code na magbibigay sa kanila ng enough power and autonomy sa future Bangsamoro Government. Nevertheless, sila yung nagsisilbing mukha ng gobyerno sa locality."

(The authenticity of autonomy that the government promised to the Bangsamoro people should have been included in the proposed Bangsamoro law. In which, the LGUs should exercise their own Local Government Code that will give them enough power and autonomy in the future Bangsamoro. Nevertheless, they are the face of the government in the locality.)

The need for the role of the negotiating panel in reaching out doesn't diminish with formal peace talks. If anything, the responsibility of the facilitators and negotiators increases after a formal peace process is established. To do so, negotiators should establish an action plan and protocol to ensure LGUs' engagement, they must enable and facilitate political and sectors in the locality — they have serve to be the voice of the voiceless minority and sectoral groups in their locality. actors to articulate and frame their concerns and demands. As with the LGUs', their realization with their significant assertions and functions in framing a Bangsamoro law help them shape their agenda to be properly engaged and have access to the negotiating panel. They certainly acknowledge that through external actors — local CSOs — ensuring the LGUs' mechanisms have sufficient resources to be able to participate and extend their leadership and managerial roles in the process. For example, most of the sectoral representatives look up to the voices and respect the opinions of the political leaders when it comes to governance and decision making related to the intergovernmental relations in the Bangsamoro, nevertheless, they also share the sentiments and concerns of the common people, minorities

"We are practically engaging with tri-people in the locality, nire-recognize po naming ang kanilang mga sentiments, positions, at concerns sa BBL. Para po ma-maintain at ma-remain naming yung "status quo" ng aming munisipyo, we recognize ourselves to be the voice of the voiceless minorities and sectors in our community. Higit pa sa lahat, at dahil na din sa suporta ng "external actors", katulad ng mga CSOs, we were able to collect and assemble the positions of the different sectors in our municipality."

(*We are practically engaging with the tri-people in the locality, we acknowledged and recognized their sentiments, positions and concerns in the BBL. So in order for us to remain and maintain the status quo of our municipality, we recognize ourselves to be the voice of the voiceless minorities and sectors in our community. Nevertheless, through the help of external actors — such as CSOs, we were able to collectively muster the positions of the different sectors in our municipality.*)

It is not just the LGUs who play an important role in the process; as so do the facilitators and external actors can play to ensure that the talks create an arena where LGUs can raise their concerns. Practically speaking, one of the second district local officials frankly narrated that LGUs have been sidelined in the consultations activities, though, the discontentment of the officials does not seem to be tangible, he elaborated that empowering LGUs', in particular, local officials like them in peace and security complexities must be one of the most important tools in a process, and using their established skills and capacities in governance can be a good starting point to make the national leaders and facilitators be aware of the importance of including them in the negotiations. One officials also added that, their the determination and practice their own authentic autonomy and governance. As he inserted in discussion:

> "Yung walang pagsuporta naming sa proseso ay lagi naming nandyan. Siguro nga ay mas nagagawa naming sumuporta behind the negotiators ngunit ang importante ngayon ay ma-realize yung sinasabing "authentic" Bangsamoro Government na kung saan yung amin right to self-determination ay ma-exercised."

> (*Our unrelenting support to the process had always been there, maybe we play significantly more behind the negotiators, but what is important right now is to realize an authentic Bangsamoro Government wherein our right to self-determination will be exercised.*)

Another participant explained that the exclusion of the LGUs' from the peace process is problematic — he emphasize that excluding the LGUs in the process, in particular, in the consultations means creating more structural deformities and systems chaos in the Bangsamoro. This means that their exclusion from the consultations will not help the spent of the BTC in crafting the proposed law. He clearly said that: facilitators to capture the difficulties, structural and system deformities, and coordination mechanisms of the regional government down to the local government, thus in order for the articulations of the LGU to be meaningfully crafted - their role as technical experts in local governance, and peace and security can be utilized and consulted on what appropriate suggestions and recommendations they can share in the facilitators in the crafting of the government. Though, generally speaking, they fully trusted the expertise and the time well

> "Sino ba naman ang maghahangad ng less autonomous na gobyerno from ARMM. Yung pag-exclude sa role ng LGUs in crafting this legislative document means foreseeing a practically deformed structure in governance, dapat maging patas at tama yung pagsali sa amin ditto sa proseso, sapagkat yung aming mga experiences in ARMM sa structure nito at mekanismo ay ma-correct sa future Bangsamoro"

> (*Who would want a less autonomous government from ARMM? Exclusion on the role of the LGUs in crafting this legislative document means foreseeing a practically deformed structure in governance, it is right and just to include us so that our experiences in the ARMM in the structure and mechanisms will be able to correct in the future Bangsamoro.*)

Basically, the role of the LGUs are very important because they are the face of the government in the locality. One of the BTC Commissioners have said that, in the Bangsamoro Basic Law, there is more coordination mechanisms between the regional government and the local government — thus, this mechanisms will be observed obediently to be able to give more exclusive powers to each government. Since the problem with the ARMM is devolution — meaning, there is an originally advancing the devolution on LGU from the national before the devolution to the ARMM. For instance, for the Internal Revenue Allotment of the LGU, the provision already did not contemplate the exercise of power of the regional government, which is why the local government is very critical. Importantly, he mentioned that the LGU will also be consulted more in the public consultations and during the establishment of the Bangsamoro government in the shaping of the local government code — because in the BBL, the parliament is authorized to come up with its own local government code to define the relationship between the regional government and the local government unit. With this, there will be a clear delineation of powers among the two set-ups, in this case, LGUs' inclusion in the consultation is very critical, and their positions and articulations must be carried out carefully in the provisions in the Basic law.

In the case of the question on how inclusive the participation of the LGUs in the peace process backflows on the different lenses on how individuals define "participation" and "inclusivity". Chang, et.al. 2015, defines participation as "the action of taking part in something" — this includes mobilization, activism, building an advocacy based social movement, form-ing coalitions, negotiation, mediation, standing for office, drafting legislation and formal agreements, holding implementers accountable, and etc. In this definition, LGUs definitely participated in the process in some way — based on LGUs perspective, as well as the understanding of the BTC. However, for Rausch and Luu 2017, they believe that to the peace process to be effective, it needs to be "inclusive and participatory". Consequently, "inclusivity" denotes the quality of trying to include many different types of people and treat them all fairly and equally (Cambridge dictionary, 2018). Yet, there are two dimensions of inclusivity, one it is identified both a practical dimension of inclusivity (inclusion as a tool for sustainable peace) and two, a more profound value dimension, which is often framed in normative terms - inclusion as a moral obligation, a question of fairness (Romo and Smeets 2015). Linking it to the experiences and involvement of the LGUs in the peace process, it is profoundly safe to say that they have been included among other sectors in the Bangsamoro, in the consultation activities both in a practical and value dimensions of inclusivity.

Nonetheless, in sum, LGUs worked in harmony to drive for better inclusion in the peace negotiations between the government of the Philippines and the MILF through unswerving public engagement, transparency, and accessibility. More so than previous peace agreements, the 2014 Comprehensive Agreement and the directives from President Duterte was remarkable for its inclusivity and sectoral representations sensitive. The case of the LGUs exhibits that a determined action resulting from participation of the LGUs in the peace talks, designated spaces and platforms for political leaders' consultations, and mass action influenced the main parties to the conflict to be more pacifying.

Implications

The lack of political space in the peace process for the LGU have been one of the considerations of the study to go further — documentation of other sectors involvement have been pursued and acknowledged in different published journals and research, however, in the case of the political sector, their participation have remained to be their own. This paper has drawn attention to the need to examine the overall experiences and involvement of the LGUs in the GPH-MILF peace process, this is to give more avenues to the peace process to have a collective analysis on what constitute an inclusive political participation, and how will "inclusivity and participation" contribute to moving the peace process forward.

Having a cohort of like-minded individuals who could push for the "home" of LGUs' issues and articulations at the very top, as seen in the representation on Commissioner Amin in the BTC, or a formal mechanism to include LGUs in political processes improved the probability of legitimatizing the peace agreement.

In the lens of Structural Functionalism Theory, the pillars being utilize in this study drawn out from the specific research questions of this paper. These four (4) pillars includes: involvement of the LGUs' in the peace process, (2) their experiences and challenges, (3) inter-LGU alliances/coordination mechanisms, and (4) LGUs' assertion on the need for political participation. Concomitantly, research findings presents that the four (4) pillars have been touched, yet still needed for further closer examination involving a lot of political actors to basically draw out a conclusion and critical analysis of the whole features of LGUs participation in the peace process. However, with the available data — given that the researcher have collected, it leads to the supporting claim of the theory that all functions and structures — which are the pillars being utilized — are functionally significant in the expression of participation of the local government units in the peace process.

Generally speaking, and based on the LGUs' narratives, they were able to mobilize their participation through advocacies, creating social movements and dialogues, involvement in consultations, and activating alliances and inter-LGU coordination mechanisms through their understanding and appreciation of their dominant roles and assertions on the need for the negotiators/facilitator to include them in the framing of a legitimate peace process. Following the principles of the used theory, the four pillars utilized are functionally necessary to describe and examined the inclusivity of LGUs participation in the process — there are narratives that

claims that somehow, the process is not that inclusive and LGUs are left out and being sidelined in the process. Yet, there are still who claims that they are equally represented by the national government since it is a government led process vis a vis an indirect representation of a former local chief executive in the BTC. In all these nuances, what matters most is the broader ownership of the political leaders to the process, and the framing of the articulations and positions of the political actors will not just leverage and influence in the negotiating table but beyond the crafting of a legislative document that buttress a workable Bangsamoro Government for all.

Consequently, entering into an agreement and creating a Bangsamoro government that would solidify and empower the Bangsamoro is intended to be a peacebuilding strategy — as such, in this kind of strategy, "inclusivity" and "participation" of all sectors in the Bangsamoro should be given an equal and fair opportunity to work together for sustainable peace. Given also that this strategy have been the only mechanism and solution for a long lasting peace in Mindanao — it is relevant to position every sentiments and issues on the inclusivity of the participation of the local government units' in the process. This in any way do not question the process and mechanisms of the negotiating panel in crafting the Bangsamoro law but to help augment some nuances that would hinder and spoil the process to move forward.

Nevertheless, LGUs have a unique role in the peace process. They are utilized mostly in the field of governance and management of peace and security aspect of a locality, among others, they also serve as the basic needs provider of the government since they are closely reach by the community. As well as, they are recognized as trusted elected political leaders that have been the source of information and critical takeaways in the current peace negotiations. Yet, with the ongoing negotiations, some maintained their "back room" roles while others are pushing for a greater access in the table — with this, like with any other groups, LGUs' have been playing crucial but relevant roles in keeping the process to be meaningfully observed and move forward. More so than the question of inclusivity, the political actors hope to visualizes a working Bangsamoro government to address the real struggle of the Bangsamoro people.

4
SUMMARY

The case of the LGUs demonstrate the diverse ways in which they are included in the peace negotiation and the whole process itself. Essentially, LGUs seized the opportunity to mobilize their genuine expression of interest and participation at a critical stage when the political space opened up to permit inclusiveness. On one hand, one narration show that the sheer presence of the LGU at the peace talks – in particular, in the BTC, is sufficient enough to guarantee of the reflection of LGUs' issues in the peace agreement. Nevertheless, this chapter contains the summary of results, recommendations, and conclusion.

The following results were evident:

1. **LGUs involvement in the GPH-MILF Peace Process** — Based on the interviews, there are two (2) perspective that have been observed, one is from the LGUs' viewpoint, while the other one is from the BTC. The first observation draws out on how complex and diverse the participation of the LGUs in the peace process, to summarize their participation, there are four (4) aspects revealed, this includes: (1) LGUs are not well represented and consulted in the peace process, since few consultations were spearheaded for their sector; (2) some believe they are equally represented through the government negotiating panel, in which, it is a government led process; (3) LGUs association and links with the MILF and/or negotiating panel had helped them gain access to the consultations and peace negotiation; and (4) LGUs have been mostly consulted and involved by the local CSOs – through invitation or partnership. However, the latter perspective ruled out that the BTC have positioned a former local chief executive and congressman, Commissioner Amin, to be the

face of the LGU in the commission. Commissioner Amin helped in the crafting of the LGUs assertions in the Bangsamoro law meaningfully.

2. **Experiences and Challenges in the Peace Process** — Ultimately, however, peace was a narrowly participatory process for LGUs. They have adopted a mechanism that would help them participate in the process – this includes joining and seizing any forums, FGDs, and RTDs organized and conducted by different agencies from the government and international and local based organizations, since this has been their long-awaited window of opportunity to engage with the people working with the crafting and ratification of the Bangsamoro Law to include their articulations and positions that will enable them to contribute in making a workable Bangsamoro government. Furthermore, they also created and initiated spaces to further ventilate their sentiments, as well as, to present their corresponding suggestions and proposals.

3. **Inter-LGU Coordination Mechanisms** — LGUs' used their personal and professional networks to build alliances and alternative inter-LGU coordination mechanisms, organize activities, and advocate their positions. Established alliances such as Iranun Inter-Agency Task Force Force, Nuling Inter-Agency Alliance, and Task Force Kapamagayun have been activated and tapped to address common issues and concerns in the peace negotiations, to tackle updates on the process and discuss further support they can extend in the negotiating panel to the process to be effective. Provincial Peace and Order Council (PPOC) is also recognize as a form of alliance, though, the aforementioned alliances and coordination mechanisms are not solely dedicated to the peace process agenda – LGU have used this links to keep themselves well-informed and to express their support in the peace process.

4. **Dominant Assertions on the need for LGUs' political participation** — For LGUs, they believed that they play a variety of roles in multifaceted, multitrack peace processes. They can sit at the formal negotiating table, on a technical working group or sub commission, or they can be exterior the talks involved as political leaders representing the LGUs in following development agendas. Furthermore, they play mostly on the level of governance and intergovernmental relations, among others, the face and frontrunners of the government in the locality. Nevertheless, they were recognized as trusted elected political leaders that have been the source of information and critical takeaways in the current peace

negotiations, though some of them are contented with their "backroom" roles, and some wanted to be empower and used their skills in governance to be utilized in the peace process.

Conclusion

This study concludes that, the logical and representative inclusion of LGUs in both parallel and horizontal lens of peace and security issues in the country, particularly in Mindanao peace process, is not solitary essential in safeguarding a successful negotiation, but also for guaranteeing that the LGUs' interests are being addressed. As such, determined action from direct participation of LGUs through the representation from the BTC in the peace talks, pressure from LGUs outside of the formal peace negotiations, and advocacy influenced the main parties to the conflict to be open-minded about LGUs' involvement in the peace process. Consequently, LGUs' used their personal connections with the negotiation panels to submit proposals for the peace agreement, provide informal moral support during critical moments of the negotiations, and update each other during consultations.

Furthermore, both the 2012 Framework Agreement and the proposed Bangsamoro Basic Law unambiguously mention local government units' several times. The provisions that shape off of the 2017 proposed Bangsamoro Basic Law plea for explicit provisions for LGUs, including their intergovernmental relations and coordination with the Bangsamoro and central government, the political participation of LGUs in the Bangsamoro, on power and functions, on local government share on natural resources and share on internal revenue tax. The dual effects of LGUs legitimately entrenched in the peace talks as well as external pressure from the civil society organization's networks influenced the language, agenda, and format of the power-sharing agreement. Yet, while LGUs participated substantively in the peace negotiations, there remains some sense that especially concerning other political leaders – who have felt being sidelined in the process, LGUs are still left out in the negotiations. Nonetheless, the LGUs view the establishment of the Bangsamoro government as largely affirmative and as they guarantee, their continuous involvement in any forms of actions will still be mobilized, in order to have a meaningful peace process and a workable Bangsamoro Government for all.

Collectively, LGUs had realize their certain and unique role in the peace process — they play mostly on the level of governance and intergovernmental relations, among others, the face and frontrunners of the government in the locality. Nevertheless, they were recognized as trusted elected political leaders that have been the source of information and critical takeaways in the current peace negotiations, though some of them are contented with their "backroom" roles, and some wanted to be empower and used their skills in governance to be utilized in the peace process.

To conclude, this research examines the inclusive participation of LGUs in the GPH- MILF peace process. The results of the study offers a rich and unique understanding of why LGUs mobilized for peace; how they organized; how they formed and activate coalitions and alliances; how they assembled and shaped agendas; how they negotiated their goals; and the scope to which the final agreement replicated the significances they championed. While this research was not compiled to evaluate the inclusivity of the process, the hope is that the lessons learned research findings and from all the narratives of the participants in total can help LGUs, the government and the negotiating panel to recognized the significance of inclusivity, particularly counting the political sectors to include their priorities codified in the peace agreements that ultimately pave the way for the next chapter in the histories of a meaningful and legitimate peace process.

Recommendations

Fundamental to the success of any peace agreement is the commitment of the implementers on the ground. Whatever might be reached by the Philippine Government and the MILF as their final agreement, the success of implementation critically hinges upon the willingness and commitment of the LGUs to implement and realize as such. The LGUs are the final implementers of the agreed provisions. It is vital to get the LGUs on-board the peace process right from the very start, as a matter of principle and logic. Therefore, this study recommends:

1) Primarily, that the membership of LGUs in the negotiating panel, the Bangsamoro Transition Commission (BTC), and the Bangsamoro Transition Authority (BTA) become an integral policy of the peace process, including their direct participation in the negotiations.

    Subsequently, the presence of LGUs can and must take numerous forms, mostly in the effort to address local peace and security, and participatory governance in the Bangsamoro. The end to these Bangsamoro struggle cannot be copied fraudulently through only a top down peace process, with only armed actors at the negotiating table. As an alternative, it necessitates a further inclusive process, one that includes the political entity playing more fundamental roles in building peace from the bottom up as well as from the top down level, through engaging multiple stakeholders in the process. Furthermore, gatherings and consultations need to be organized not just in the capital city but also at the local level where the communities are challenged with a multitude of perilous concerns that left unaddressed could disentangle any peace deal.

2) Secondly, the peace process special bodies on security, such as the Joint Normalization Committee, Joint Peace and Security Team (JPST), and the Third Party Monitoring Team (TPMT) be institutionalized in the security mechanisms and structure of the LGU or the provincial government. This include their membership in the Provincial Peace and Order Council (PPOC), or the Municipal Peace and Order Council. This way, the operational link binding the special bodies with local government structure is ensured and strengthened, towards forging of inclusive peace for the Bangsamoro.

Furthermore, to provide a safe passage mechanisms of any peace process to be implemented meaningfully, the following ought to be considered:

1) Ensure a political environment that values contribution of all sector, in particular the Local Government units to good governance, and peace and security developments.
2) Support existing or newly established 'local machineries' for LGUs' empowerment or inclusion in the peace process by strengthening existing partnerships and forged new ones – this will help in bringing the table within the reach of the sectors in the community.
3) Support LGUs and CSOs with their initiatives and creation of spaces/platform for the ventilation of their sentiments and articulations in the implementation of peace agreements and lobby for the implementation of demands for inclusive process.
4) Support awareness-raising and sensitization campaigns through decentralized, local government units' networks, which inform about the aims of peace processes and address common articulations on the sector.
5) Establish clearer roles for the LGUs to meaningfully participate and involve in the process.

6) Clarify and define the representation of the LGUs, and other sector in the ongoing peace process to elicit any feeling of sidelined and unrepresented in the negotiating panel.
7) Partner with the Regional and Local Government Units in efforts to strengthen inter-LGUs dialogue, capacities and cooperation towards translation of peace agreements to a workable policy and law.

Recommendations for Further Studies

There are a number of facets of involvements and case studies that the researcher would like to further examine. With limited time and resources, the researcher chose to focus exclusively on the Local Government Units' inclusive participation in the GPH-MILF Process. However, it would be beneficial to the process and other context of process in the inside and outside the country to further check the following:

1) In-depth exploration of how Local Government Units committed to peace process involvement and how they have been influenced by the internal and external actors in the negotiations. Further research might compare, for example, the internal versus the external influences and/or factor in their participation. Research could explore the LGUs in the 5 provinces of Autonomous Region in Muslim Mindanao, and identify what could have been the common challenges and push factor of the LGUs participation in the current process.
2) Examination on the need to investigate the reasons why the LGU are not included in the peacemaking.
3) More methodological work is needed on how to robustly capture the impact and outcomes of entering into the peace agreement and negotiations analysis and exploration of the impact of peace process in the local peace and security context in the LGUs.
4) Research to develop approaches and carry out what makes an inclusive peace process to work out. Although methodologically challenging, it would be very advantageous to conduct some longer-term studies which sought to quantify the impact of the participation of each sector – women, Civil Society Organizations, Indigenous People, Sultanate, political actors, and etc.—in the formulation of a workable Bangsamoro Government.
5) It would also be helpful to capture qualitatively the experiences and perspectives of Bangsamoro sectoral representatives who have had mixed

or negative experiences. Similarly, further research might explore the (relatively rare) experiences of marginalised and seldom-heard groups involved in peace process.

6) A final relatively narrow but significant research would be on the "Lessons Learned by the Negotiating Panel and the Bangsamoro People to the whole process on granting the groups' aspirations in pursuit to the exercise of self-determination in the Bangsamoro community".

APPENDICES

APPENDIX A
KEY INFORMANT INTERVIEW (KII) AND FOCUS GROUP DISCUSSION GUIDE QUESTIONS

Name			
Age		Sex	☐ Male ☐ Female
Designation			
Municipality			

- How are the LGUs involved in the GPH-MILF peace process?
  - Specifically:
    a) Are LGUs being consulted? How?
    b) Are LGUs being invited in the dialogue and forums related to the peace process?
    c) Are LGUs recommendations and assertions included and heard?
    d) Are LGUs well represented in consultations and dialogues?
    e) Are you convinced that the LGUs are being heard or consulted during the peace negotiations?
    f) Are you convinced that the LGUs suggestions and recommendations are being considered?

- What are the prevailing experiences and challenges of the Local Government Units' participation in the peace negotiations?
  - Specifically:
    a) What have been the LGUs experiences related to the peace process?
    b) What have you considered as the great obstacle of your participation in the peace process?
    c) How does the LGU take part in consultations, dialogues and forum?
    d) How often do LGUs being consulted?
    e) Who always consult and/or reach out with the LGUs?

- f) Does the LGU conduct Peace and Security Council meetings and gatherings in support to the current peace track?

▶ How does the inter-LGU coordination influence in terms of asserting their participation in the peace process?
  ▷ Specifically:
    a) Are there any existing LGU coordinating formations in the area in support to the peace negotiation? If yes, how was it formed? Who initiated the formations?
    b) Are there challenges in inter-LGU coordination in terms of their participation in the peace negotiation?

▶ What are the dominant assertions on the need for LGUs' political participation in the peace process?
  ▷ Specifically:
    a) What are the important roles of LGUs in the peace negotiations?
    b) What are the advantages of LGUs participation in the peace process? Why?
    c) Is there any disadvantages on the need for LGUs participation in the peace process? If yes, what are these? Why?

APPENDIX B
DATA COLLECTION AND PROCEDURE FLOW CHART

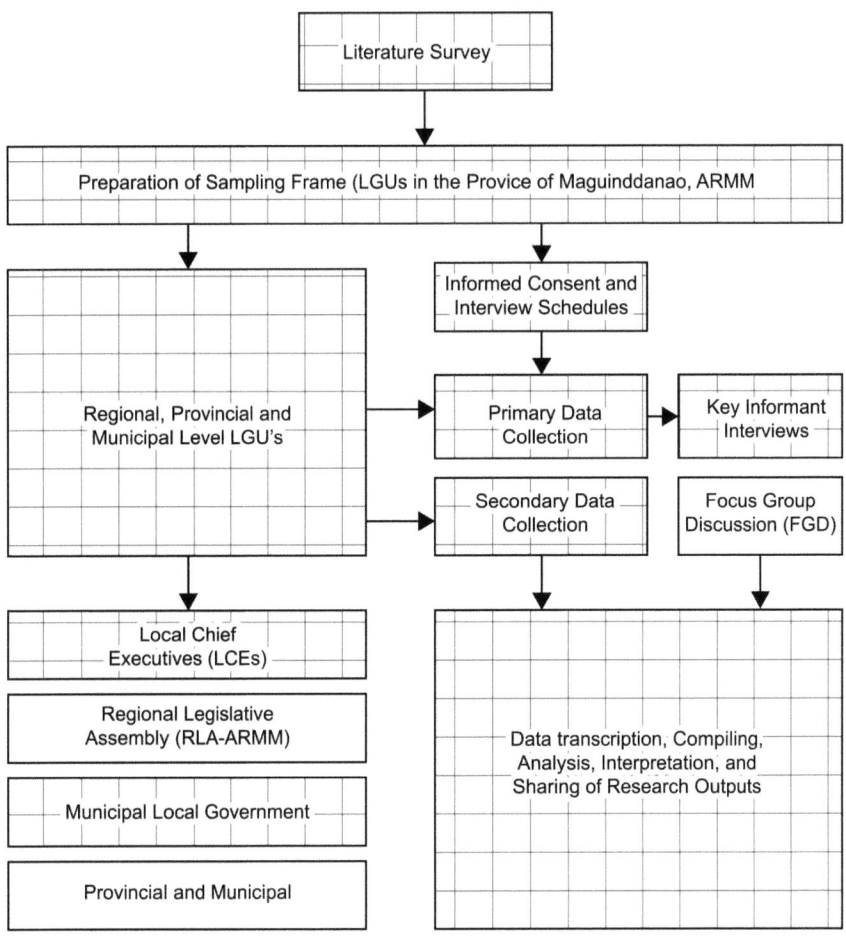

APPENDIX C
DATA CAPTURE PLAN FOR RESEARCH

Objective	Data Needed	Questions to Ask

To be able to identify the nature of LGUs' inclusive participation and involvement in the GPH-MILF Peace Process.	△ Activities and Forums participation
	△ Consultations and Dialogue association
	△ Community-based peace processes and mechanisms
	△ Informed support and ownership of LGUs of current peace process.
		▶ How are the LGUs involved in the GPH-MILF peace process?
		   ▽ Specifically:
		   a) Are LGUs being consulted? How?
		   b) Are LGUs being invited in the dialogue and forums related to the peace process?
		   c) Are LGUs recommendations and assertions included and heard?
		   d) Are LGUs well represented in consultations and dialogues?
		   e) Are you convinced that the LGUs are being heard or consulted during the peace negotiations?
		   f) Are you convinced that the LGUs suggestions and recommendations are being considered?
		   g) How does the LGU take part in consultations, dialogues and forum?
		   h) How often do LGUs being consulted?
		   i) Who always consult and/or reach out with the LGUs?
		   j) Does the LGU conduct Peace and Security Council meetings and gatherings in support to the current peace track?

Objective	Data Needed	Questions to Ask
To determine the manifestations of inter-LGU coordination pertaining to peace process issues	▵ Nature of inter-LGU coordination ▵ Formed partnerships and coalitions ▵ Process of inter-LGU Coordination	▲ How does the inter-LGU coordination influence in terms of asserting their participation in the peace process? △ Specifically: a) Are there any existing LGU coordinating formations in the area in support to the peace negotiation? If yes, how was it formed? Who initiated the formations? b) Are there challenges in inter-LGU coordination in terms of their participation in the peace negotiation?
To locate dominant assertions on the need for LGUs' political participation in the peace process	▵ Important Roles of LGUs in the peace process ▵ Significance of LGUs participation in the peace process	▲ What are the dominant assertions on the need for LGUs' political participation in the peace process? △ Specifically: a) What are the important roles of LGUs in the peace negotiations? b) What are the advantages of LGUs participation in the peace process? Why? c) Is there any disadvantages on the need for LGUs participation in the peace process? If yes, what are these? Why?

APPENDIX D
LETTER OF APPOINTMENT

(Date)
_____
_____

Dear_____,

Assalamu Alaikum!

In partial fulfilment of my requirements for my Master's Degree Dissertation entitled **"The examination of the Local Government Units' Participation in the GPH-MILF Peace Process"**, I would like to provide you with more information about this study and what your involvement would entail if you decide to take part. Said study aims to review the state of art on the LGUs' participation in peace negotiations thus providing an overview on how they have been involved and engaged in the broader lens of peace making in the country, particularly, their participation in the evolving Mindanao Peace Process. This study will be conducted under the supervision of Prof. Rey Dan Lacson of the Institute for Autonomy and Governance (IAG). In connection with this, may I seek an appointment with you this Tuesday, February 6, 2018, 2:00 in the afternoon in your office, for an in-depth conversation on the following matters:

1. Prevailing experiences and challenges of the LGUs' participation in the peace negotiations
2. LGUs' nature of involvement in political decision-making within the Mindanao Peace Process in terms of nature and extent of influence.
3. Inter-LGU coordination in terms of asserting their participation in the peace process
4. Dominant assertions on the need for LGUs' political participation in the peace process

I hope that the results of my study will be of benefit to those organizations directly involved in the study, other voluntary recreation organizations not directly involved in the study, as well as to the broader research community.

I very much look forward to speaking with you and thank you in advance for your assistance in this project.

Sincerely Yours,
HAZELYN GAUDIANO, RN
MAPD Student, Notre Dame University

APPENDIX E
RESPONDENT CONSENT FORM

I, Ms. Hazelyn Gaudiano will be conducting a study on the "The examination of the Local Government Units' Participation in the GPH-MILF Peace Process". All data generated from this interview will be used to advocate for policies and programs on ensuring the inclusivity and participation of all sectors in the Bangsamoro proposed government. Rest assured that all information in this interview will be kept with utmost confidentiality.

TO BE COMPLETED BY THE PARTICIPANT.

▷ I have read the information sheet about this study
▷ I have had an opportunity to ask questions and discuss this study
▷ I have received satisfactory answers to all my questions
▷ I have received enough information about this study
▷ I understand that I am / the participant is free to withdraw from this study.
▷ I understand that my research data may be used for a further project in anonymous form, but I am able to opt out of this if I so wish, by ticking here.
▷ I agree to take part in this study

Signed (participant)	Date
Full Name:	

REFERENCES

Alim, Guiamel (2000). *The Bangsamoro Struggle for Self-Determination.* Retrieved from http://www.seasite.niu.edu/tagalog/modules/modules/muslimmindanao/bangsamoro_ struggle_for_self.htm

AUSA (Association of the U. S. Army) and CSIS (Center for Strategic and International Studies) (2002). *Post-Conflict Reconstruction: Task Framework.* CSIS and AUSA. Retrieved from https://csis- prod.s3.amazonaws.com/s3fspublic/legacy_files/files/media/csis/pubs/framework.pdf

Bacani, Benedicto (2008). *Editorial.* In B.B., E. Mercado, S. Ambolodto, Z. Malang, A. Rasul & K. Preschle (Eds), The Mindanao Peace Process: Issues and Challenges (pp.5). Cotabato City, Philippines: Institute for Autonomy and Governance.

Batas Pinoy (2011, April 5). *Definition and functions of LGU.* Retrieved from https://bataspinoy.wordpress.com/2011/04/05/definition-and-functions-of-lgu/

Burgess, Heidi (2004). *Peace Processes.* Retrieved from https://www.beyondintractability.org/essay/peace_processes

CANA, no date, *Citizens Primer,* "What to Know about Your LGU?. Retrieved from http://citizenaction.net/images/LGU-PRIMER-CANA-COLORED-FINAL.pdf

Chang, Patty, Alam, Mayesha, Warren, Roslyn, Bhatia, Rukmani & Turkington, Rebecca (2015). *Women Leading Peace: A close examination of women's political participation in peace processes* (pp. 17–31). In M. Verveer (Ed). Washington D.C, USA: Georgetown Institute for Women, Peace and Security.

Conciliation Resources (2015). *"Operationalizing women's meaningful participation' in the Bangsamoro."* Retrieved from http://www.c-r.org/resources/operationalising-womensmeaningful-participation-bangsamoro

Copus, Colin (2013). *The Role of Local Governance in Europe.* In W. Hofmeister, M. Sarmah and P. Rüppel. Local Politics and Governance (pp. 39–50). Singapore: Konrad- Adenauer Stiftung Ltd

Ferrer, Miriam Coronel (2016). *Forging Peace Settlement for the Bangsamoro: Compromises and Challenges*. In P. Hutchcroft (Ed), Mindanao the Long Journey to Peace and Prosperity (pp. 99–133). Mandaluyong City, Philippines: Anvil Publishing, Inc.

Gormley-Heenan, Cathy (2007). *Political Leadership and the Northern Ireland Peace Process*. Retrieved from http://www.palgrave.com/us/book/9780230 500372#reviews.

Government of the Philippines, no date. *The Constitution of the Republic of the Philippines*. Retrieved from https://ppp.gov.ph/wp-content/uploads /2015/01/The-Local- Government-Code-of-the-Philippines.pdf .

Herbolzheimer, Kristian (2015). *The peace process in Mindanao, the Philippines: Evolution and Lessons Learned*. Retrieved from Norwegian Peacebuilding Resource Centre (NOREF). URL: http://www.c-r.org/downloads/a6c4f73 39db9c90cd15a63c85405404e.pdf

International Centre for Parliamentary Studies Ltd, no date. *Governance*. Retrieved from http://www.parlicentre.org/Governance.php

Institute for Autonomy and Governance (2014). *Policy Report: Transitioning Bureaucracy from ARMM to Bangsamoro*. Retrieved from: http://iag.org. ph/index.php/blog/478- policy-report-transitioning-bureaucracy-from-armm-to-bangsamoro

Institute for Autonomy and Governance (2014). *What Ails ARMM*. Retrieved from: https://iag2001.wordpress.com/policy-brief/what-ails-armm/

Institute for Autonomy and Governance (2011). *Policy Report: Enhancing regional-LGU relations*. Retrieved from: http://iag.org.ph/index.php/blog /483-policy-report- enhancing-regional-lgu-relations

Knack, Paula Defensor (2014). *Bangsamoro Peace Deal for Mindanao: Where's the Peace?*. Retrieved from The Diplomat. URL: http://thediplomat. com/2014/04/bangsamoro- peace-deal-for-mindanao-wheres-the-peace/

Lacson, Rey Danilo (2017). *Foreword*. In R.D.L (Ed), Working Papers on Local Governance for the Evolving Bangsamoro (p. 3). Cotabato City, Philippines: Pro PolitiCS for Peace Project-Institute for Autonomy and Governance.

Lingga, Abhoud Syed (2016). *Building the Bangsamoro Government*. In P. Hutchcroft (Ed), Mindanao the Long Journey to Peace and Prosperity (pp. 133–159). Mandaluyong City, Philippines: Anvil Publishing, Inc.

Lingga, Abhoud (2002). *Democratic Approach to Pursue the Bangsamoro People's Right to Self-determination.* Retrieved from http://democracy.mkolar.org/Bangsamoro-Self-Determination.html

Lorena, Jose (2017). Interview on *"Reformatted Bangsamoro draft law ready for submission to Congress".* Retrieved from http://www.philstar.com/headlines/2017/06/17/1710929/reformatted-bangsamoro-draft-law-ready-submission-congress

Macionis, John and Gerber, Linda (2010). *Sociology 7th Canadian Ed.* (pp 14). Canada: Pearson Canada Inc.

Meen, Madhang Majok (2017). *Religious and Political Leaders in Gok Urged to Champion Peace Talks.* Retrieved from https://reliefweb.int/report/south-sudan/religious-and-political-leaders-gok-urged-champion-peace-talks

Mercado, Eliseo (1999). *Southern Philippines Question (challenge of Peace and Development).* Cotabato City, Philippines: Notre Dame University.

Office on the Presidential Adviser on Peace Process (OPAPP) (2015). *OPAPP sets record straight: More than 550 consultations on Bangsamoro peace process done by GPH panel alone.* Retrieved from: http://archive.peace.gov.ph/milf/news/opapp-sets-record- straight-more-550-consultations-bangsamoro-peace-process-done-gph-panel

OPAPP, UNDP (2013). *Guidebook on Conflict-Sensitive and Peace-Promoting Local Development Planning.* Retrieved from: file:///C:/Users/Hazel%20Gaudiano/Downloads/CSSP_Coverpage%20(2).pdf

Paffenholz, Thania (2014). *Broadening participation in peace processes Dilemmas & options for mediators* (pp. 13–23). Geneva, Switzerland: Centre for Humanitarian Dialogue. Retrieved from http://www.hdcentre.org/wp-content/uploads/2016/07/MPS4 Broadening participation-in-peace-processes-July-2014.pdf

Rausch, Colette; and Luu, Tina (2017). *Inclusive Peace Processes Are Key to Ending Violent Conflict.* Retrieved from https://www.usip.org/publications/2017/05/inclusive-peace-processes-are-key-ending-violent-conflict

Romo, Pablo and Smeets, Marylene (2015). *Inclusivity in Mediation Processes: Lessons from Chiapas* (pp. 6–8). In V. Sticher (Ed). Mediation Support Network. Retrieve from: http://www.css.ethz.ch/content/dam/ethz/special-interest/gess/cis/center-for-securities-studies/pdfs/MSN_Discussion_Points.pdf

Santiago, Irene (2015). *The Participation of Women in the Mindanao Peace Process*. Retrieved from:http://www.unwomen.org//media/headquarters/attachments/sections/library/publications/2017/participation-of-women-in-mindanao-peace process.pdf?la=en&vs=3030

Saunders, Harold (1999). A Public Peace Process: Sustained Dialogue to Transform Racial and Ethnic Conflict.New York: St. Martin's Press. Retrieved from: https://journals.lib.unb.ca/index.php/jcs/article/view/4343/4988

Senate of the Philippines (2007). *Gordon says ARMM needs real fiscal autonomy*. Retrieved from: https://www.senate.gov.ph/press_release/2007/0825_gordon2.asp

Suazo, Adan .E. (2013). *Tools of Change: Long-Term Inclusion in Peace Processes*. Fletcher Journal of Humanity Security, XXVIII: PP.5 -23. Retrieved from: *https://www.cmi.no/file/2633-Lasting-PeaceTiitmamerAwolich.pdf*

Tayao, Edmund (2017). *In Search for Autonomy and Good Governance towards a Functioning Regional Government for Muslim Mindanao* (pp. 7–21). Cotabato City, Philippines: Pro PolitiCS for Peace Project-Institute for Autonomy and Governance.

Uson, John Felix (2017, June 17). *Reformatted Bangsamoro draft law ready for submission to Congress*. Retrieved from http://www.philstar.com/headlines/2017/06/17/1710929/reformatted-bangsamoro-draft-law-ready-submission-congress